The
PURPOSE
PRINCIPLES

The
PURPOSE
PRINCIPLES

How to Draw More
Meaning into Your Life

Jake Ducey

JEREMY P. TARCHER/PENGUIN

a member of Penguin Group (USA)

New York

JEREMY P. TARCHER/PENGUIN
Published by the Penguin Group
Penguin Group (USA) LLC
375 Hudson Street
New York, New York 10014

USA · Canada · UK · Ireland · Australia
New Zealand · India · South Africa · China

penguin.com
A Penguin Random House Company

Most Tarcher/Penguin books are available at special quantity discounts for
bulk purchase for sales promotions, premiums, fund-raising, and educational
needs. Special books or book excerpts also can be created to fit specific needs.
For details, write: Special.Markets@us.penguingroup.com.

ISBN 978-0-399-17264-9

Printed in the United States of America
10 9 8 7 6 5 4 3 2 1

Book design by Ellen Cipriano

This book is dedicated to one of my first heroes, my brother, Cole Patrick Ducey.

I also dedicate this book to Inga and Jack—I never would've had the inspiration to write this had it not been for your support.

CONTENTS

FOREWORD

The circumstances surrounding my first meeting with Jake Ducey illustrate some of the reasons why I wanted to write this foreword.

It was 2013 and I was emceeing a fund-raising event in Los Angeles. The event was sold out and the ballroom was full. Someone had told Jake that I would be speaking there, so he bought a last-minute ticket in the hopes of meeting me. He was twenty years old and was about to publish his first book, *Into the Wind*, which he said was inspired by me. He drove two and a half hours to the event carrying a signed copy of his book for me. His sole intention was to introduce himself and give me the book. But the odds were slim considering how crowded the event was.

Toward the end of the night I went to my seat for dinner. That was when Jake walked over to introduce himself.

"Hi, Jack. I am Jake Ducey. I wrote this book and you inspired it," he said.

"How did I inspire it?" I asked.

"You say in your book *The Success Principles* that when someone says 'No,' you say 'Next.' And every time I was told I was too young to be an author, or when literary agents told me I needed more experience before they would represent me, I just kept saying 'Next,' and I didn't quit. Now I am standing here with you, holding my book!" Jake said this with a zest for life I came to appreciate quickly.

My face lit up with a smile. I could feel passion oozing out of him. I immediately welcomed him and introduced my wife. While the waiters served dinner at my table, Jake and my wife chatted. Coincidentally, his mom and my wife went to the same high school. But what was more of a coincidence was that in that sold-out event, where there seemed to be no empty seats, the chair to my left was somehow empty. Once the food was placed in front of us, I asked Jake if he was going to sit there and enjoy the plate of food at the empty seat next to me. He said he was so excited he hadn't noticed that the chair was empty!

What are the chances? What are the odds that out of a five-hour event, where there seemed to be no empty seats, Jake got the urge to come introduce himself at the exact moment the waiter was coming to serve dinner at my table—and that the person next to me had left early? How is it possible that the opportunity for us to connect happened so perfectly?

I believe it was possible because of Jake's belief. He says he didn't know "how" he would meet me—he just knew it was possible that we'd become friends.

A few months later, my wife and I invited him to my birthday party. That evening he asked me, "Jack, what do I need to know in life to live my dreams?"

"Write it down, make it happen," I told him.

He sat there, hoping I would explain myself in more detail.

"Jake, you have within you the ability to achieve anything you desire, because if you didn't, you wouldn't be able to have the desire in the first place," I said.

A few months after my birthday, Jake wrote me to let me know he followed my advice, and that Tarcher/Penguin would be publishing his new book, *The Purpose Principles*, which was inspired by our chat and by my book *The Success Principles*.

As I have become older, one of my passions is inspiring and empowering young people to live their highest vision through the Success Principles seminars I conduct. One of those Success Principles is "Ask for What You Want." I believe that everything you want is out there waiting for you to ask for it.

Just as Jake illustrates in this book, your dreams aren't out of reach, your fears and limiting beliefs don't have to stop you, and you're never too young or too old to live more confidently or to make a difference. You are fully capable of waking up every day to a more productive and meaningful life by simply choosing to apply these principles!

Jake considers me his mentor—a role I relish. Just as important, I consider him an inspiration in my life. Jake is such a radiant and inspirational being because he has chosen to live a life committed to the full expression of his unlimited potential. And because of that, he has the ability to inspire others to live their dreams, too. I am confident that through this book Jake will now inspire you to achieve *your* most heartfelt dreams, and by so doing, contribute to a more equitable, just, and compassionate world.

—*Jack Canfield*

coauthor of The Success Principles *and*
the Chicken Soup for the Soul series

A WORD FROM THE AUTHOR

From the beginning of time, billions of people have dreamed about living meaningfully. Some even dream about changing the world, or at least their own one. Though most of us *do* dream, few of us *live* our dreams. Many of us simply can't uncover *how* to do so.

The ability to live our dreams is the great mystery. Why do some people seem so skillful and impassioned, while others can't step out of the choking monotony of an ordinary existence? This book was written to answer this question and others, including: How can we live a meaningful life? How does one become more successful, confident, and fulfilled? What do the world's most successful, happy, and influential people have in common? What common attitudes, traits, beliefs, and strategies do those who've marked human history share? How can one simply live with more joy?

In this book you'll find common principles, characteristics, beliefs, and stories that have helped some of the greatest contributors and achievers of the twenty-first century. These ideas can be used to improve your internal world as well as the world around you. Each and every chapter provides a stimulus to help you find a deeper meaning in your life, find passion in simple things (such as the beauty of the sky), and even find ways to alter the course of human history.

While in the process of uncovering these keys, you'll find it easy to dismiss any feelings of doubt that you may have had when starting this book. If you've ever tried and failed, had difficulties that kept you from getting what you want, or found that your progress has been stunted by illness or physical ailments, these stories may prove to be the very thing you'll need to overcome your obstacles.

If you are *committed* to putting these principles to work, you'll no longer see yourself as anything less than those mentioned throughout the book. I could tell you how you'll know when you've reached this state of inner strength, but that would deprive you of much of the value that you'll receive when you make your own discoveries. And if you're thinking, "I am *not* meant to live the life I love," or, "I *can't* change the world," then please consider this question: "If not *you*, then *who*?"

It's important to note that education and age have *nothing* to do with your ability to make an impact. A college dropout named Steve Jobs applied these principles to alter the course of human history with his technological inventions and the creation of Apple. High school dropout and founder of Virgin, Richard Branson, used these principles to build one of the largest business enterprises in history. A degreeless Malcolm X used the knowledge herein to find the strength, clarity, and know-how to alter the course of human history and bring about greater racial equality. And Mother Teresa, an uneducated (at least by formal standards) woman from a small town in Macedonia, also lived these principles and transformed the consciousness of the Western world.

You'll find their stories and lessons throughout the book alongside many others. My goal is to show you that a deeply fulfilling life charged with purpose, contribution, and success is obtainable by applying the knowledge learned herein. The subtitle of this book is *How to Draw More Meaning into Your Life*. I chose the word *draw* because it has a double meaning and it is often associated with artists. Drawing is a creative act that requires vision, imagination, originality, dedication, and patience. It is a perfect metaphor for the way we need to approach life. We must apply our artistic skills to get the most out of each day. An artist doesn't stop at seeing a vision or having an idea in their mind—they take it further and work to turn what they've seen in their imagination into reality. This is the same skill set that needs to be developed in those who want to live an authentic life of *their own* creation.

How do I know that this works? You'll be answering that question on your own before you're done with this book. You may find the answer in the first chapter, or perhaps on the last page.

To you loving your life,
Jake Ducey

INTRODUCTION

February 7, 2013

He was standing with a beautiful, tan young woman when I saw him. He had a big smile on his face. I could see his friendly blue eyes glint in the warm San Diego sun. That's when he opened his arms to give me a welcoming hug. He was walking out the door of the Counter, a burger joint next door to Jimbo's Natural Foods in Encinitas, San Diego, where I was going to grab some groceries. I had just parked my car and was walking a few hundred feet along the sidewalk to the store.

"Jake, congratulations on your book! I can't wait to get a copy. You inspire me!" he said with enthusiasm.

He made me feel so good about myself when he said it. So good that I told him to wait there on the sidewalk while I went back to my car to grab him a copy that I had in my trunk. I signed it for him:

Dear Vic,
With love for doing what you love while you're alive.
Love,
Jake

We gave each other a hug. I could tell by his genuine excitement for the book that he'd read it soon, perhaps even that very day. Five hours later I got a phone call from my best friend, Luke. "Hey man," he said, "I hope you're sitting down. . . . Vic just died. He was skateboarding without a helmet on, hit his head, and died on impact."

I was shocked. I feel that I deal pretty well with death, but Vic's really hit me. Especially because the book that I had just gifted him, *Into the Wind*, relayed the message that you can die at any time, which is why it is important to *live* now. And yet, there he went, onward and outward from this physical experience.

A few days later, about 350 people showed up for his celebration of life. I can still see his brother Charlie's tears falling as he stood next to me. My friendship with Charlie had dwindled since high school—he joined the army and I distanced myself from organizational structures. We didn't seem to have much in common anymore. But on that day we shared something that connected us again. Death showed both of us that life must be lived as we want it to be lived—that it was to have *meaning*—for it will soon be gone. Perhaps even abruptly.

I saw his mom soon afterward. She said Vic had read my book from the moment I gave it to him until right before the time of his accident. That made me cry. I knew he'd read the opening quote from the book, a quote from Steve Jobs, "Remembering I'll be dead soon is the most important tool that I've ever encountered to help me make the big choices in life." I wondered if my book had cursed him or set him free. I assumed that after he read it he was inspired to go and do what he loved—skateboard.

Later, I learned that he had left a page bookmarked where he'd been reading, as if he was planning to be back to finish it soon . . . or perhaps his subconscious wanted to mark the last page that he ever read. I walked away from the celebration of life crying and asking myself, "Is it better to die young and brave the adventure, or to live long and weather the sun of comfort and security, having never really lived?"

This also makes me think about some of the last words of my good friend's father, Loren Nancarrow, who passed away after a long battle with cancer on December 28, 2013: "One of the lessons I've learned in life is that happiness lies in discovering your passions and exploring them fiercely. And passions aren't necessarily big, grand notions. We can also find passion in a rose garden, in the smell of a puppy, and the writing of a first grader. Wherever they are, whatever they may be, seek out your passions and cultivate them."

This is so true. And unfortunately so few of us spend time cultivating our passions. . . .

Chapter 1

Seeing Without Eyes

The only thing worse than being blind is having sight but no vision.

—HELEN KELLER

"I just want to thank you," a gray-haired, well-dressed man said to me. "This is the first time in my life I've ever known what I wanted because this is the first time I've ever been asked what I *really* want. . . ."

I looked at the man. He was dressed in a nice suit and looked like he was doing quite well financially. There was a brightness in his eyes that continued to speak on his behalf. "Heck, I've made good money, but my life has only been average because I've done what everyone wanted me to do ever since I can remember. Now I'm sixty-one years old, and I finally know what I want from life!"

I was shocked. This happened at the end of one of my all-day workshops where I help people define their vision and create a plan to achieve it. I truly believe that we must find what we really want, and not simply get stuck doing what we think we're supposed to do. So there I was, a twenty-one-year-old college dropout, with a man almost triple my age standing in front of me telling me that he'd never known what he *really* wanted out of life—that he'd never been deeply fulfilled with his lifestyle, regardless of the fact that he'd made good money.

The craziest thing of all is that he's not alone. Most of us don't know what we want, and haven't been given the time and space to find clarity about it. It isn't something we're taught in school. As a default, we gravitate to what's considered normal and easy—what our parents, friends, spouses, and bosses want from us. Yet when we're little we're told stories about the legends and visionaries: Martin Luther King Jr., Mahatma Gandhi, Steve Jobs, Rosa Parks, Anne Frank, Abraham Lincoln, Michael Jordan, and other seemingly larger-than-life people.

We've developed a romantic affair with the word *visionary*. But we often fail to ask the questions: *How* did they get there? What do they all have in common? When did they become so great? Where did their ability to alter human history come from? Why them?

Instead of digging deeper to answer these questions, we naively tell our kids stories about honorable people by making them out to be some rare breed of superior humans. Ones that are born with gifts that you and I don't have. What intrigues me about all the visionaries that I mentioned above (and others, including Aristotle, Maya Angelou, Plato, Albert Einstein, and Mark Twain) is the fact that they continued to breathe the same air as us. Has that ever occurred to you? The very same sun warmed their bodies. They watched the same stars. Anatomically, they were the same. They used two feet when they walked. *And* they were really weird— seriously, very strange. But all of us are odd in our own ways, so that can't be the sole reason they've become legendary, rather than ordinary.

These people aren't really unique on any level except one: they knew exactly what they wanted. They had a vision. They put this vision before their very lives, and, thus, became larger than life. But let's not get captured in the Hollywood shindig of the lights, icons, and cult-like following of celebrities—let's stick with how these people made lives filled with such meaning and value. The first place to focus our attention is *vision*: knowing what you want.

They knew that life is too short to live without dreams and to do any nonsense that you don't want to do. There's no point to life if you don't find what you love and then work toward that vision every day. One day you will (or perhaps won't) wake up and there won't be time to do all that you wanted to do—that's why the greats became great; they knew this and did what they loved while they still could.

You and I (and everyone else who has ever breathed earth's air) are like individual planets. Each of us has a gravitational pull. The women and men who've changed the world knew that if you decide and define what you want to pull into your life, and know the destiny you want to orbit in, the moons that shine on your night will be those of a meaningful life.

However, before this can happen you must know what you desire. Some people may think, "That sounds a lot like the Law of Attraction," the New Age philosophy that says by simply thinking about what you want, it comes to you—no work required. But it's not—what I am talking about is the law of refusing to subject yourself to someone else's agenda, knowing what you want out of life, seeing the vision, and getting it through lots of hustle, no matter the cost. There's nothing mystical about it. Every great person knew first what he or she wanted, and then achieved it through hard work.

The problem that 97 percent of the population has is that they don't know what they want, or they have never even thought about what they want. They unconsciously pull the wants, needs, and opinions of others into their orbit—they follow the popular trends and fads that are suggested to them by the media. If one doesn't choose, it's chosen for them. What they unconsciously pull into their lives as their daily routine—the people who surround them, and everything else that their experience entails—is largely created by default. Then one day they say, "Hey! This isn't what I want! What I am doing?" Many of us submit to what our parents, friends, teachers, Hollywood stars, and others tell us we're supposed to do. When we don't question what they say, we unconsciously accept it, believing they must know best. Year after year it's pounded into us: *you should be this, you should do that, you're best at this, this is the smartest decision for you.*

We start to believe that we want what others want for us, which was the case of the man I met and told you about earlier. Or at least that was his case prior to the day it dawned on him in my workshop. That day he realized that he didn't want what he had—he wanted something more. Unfortunately, most of us aren't aware that we don't want to do what we're doing. We're too busy being distracted by pretty, tasty, entertaining, and mind-altering things. We're so busy that we don't have time to wonder why we're running around so much. We're too distracted to feel our own feelings.

People often say, "I *think* I feel this. . . ." Can you see that that's where we've lost? We've started to overthink how we feel. We think about what we want rather than just feeling out and doing the thing that gives our life the most excitement and meaning.

That's why people thought Steve Jobs was crazy—he quit doing what he thought he should do and started doing what he felt he should do. And everyone said, "What are you thinking? Don't drop out of college!"

But he wasn't thinking—he was feeling. He answered the inner calling of destiny and purpose that lies within each of us. People also questioned the Wright brothers when they said they would make a plane fly. But they felt that they could and they did.

It's actually quite funny. We've thought up our entire reality (what's good and bad, right and wrong, smart and dumb, safe and risky, normal and crazy, possible and impossible), but we've never considered the most important thing—what we want. Instead, we've just created boundaries around everything and have decided that this is how life is supposed to be lived.

But how can anyone tell you what your life is supposed to be like? How can another person decide how you're going to spend your time when they aren't you? The answer is that it's possible only if we give up our power of choice. But no legend, visionary, or hero has ever done that. They don't give up their right to decide their own destiny. The old adage "Live your life" simply means *live your life*. It does not mean: "Live Mommy's life," or "Live Daddy's life that he never had the courage to live," or "Live Justin Bieber's life," or "Live the life that everyone else says you should live," or "Live the life of what's easiest and most normal," or "Live the life that your teachers tell you is right, smart, and safe." "*Live your life*" means live your *own* life, and nobody else's.

To make this happen you must take the first step in living the life you want, which is to create the terms of your life. You must have a dream—a direction. However, this is often the moment when a voice in our heads creeps in and says, *What if people think I am crazy?*

When this happens you need to reason with your mind and say, "Who cares if people think I'm nuts? It's better to be strange to others than to be a stranger to myself." Be yourself—whoever that is. And that is only possible if you don't settle until you find what you love and do it with all of your heart and focus!

One of the most quoted lines in literature is Shakespeare's "To be, or not to be: that is the question. . . ." Rather than "that is the question," I would say, "that is the choice." A choice we all have to make—to be the person you want to be and do the things you really want to do, or make the choice not to. When you choose to pursue what you love, life becomes so much more than what we think of as ordinary experiences, choices, routines, and careers.

Despite the fact that I am a college dropout, I believe that I have the educational understanding to give you a thesis on the first step in living above and beyond the ordinary—*know what you want*. That's it. And when you know what you want, you know what you will or won't stand for. The greats that I mentioned above wouldn't stand for anything other than what they wanted, and that's why they changed history. That's why we talk about them and all the lives they've touched.

The only difference between social icons and the average person is that they knew what they wanted—they had a vision and a direction, something that pulled them out of bed. They didn't listen to the voice in their heads that said, "Turn the alarm off and go back to sleep for another fifteen minutes and then get out of bed and get to work!" We've all had *that voice* get us out of bed . . . but, come on, is that really the voice we want to wake up to? No!

Still, that is why most heart attacks occur between the hours of 6:00 a.m. and 9:00 a.m. on Monday mornings. Stress, worry, fear, and boredom pull people out of bed, when they deserve to be pulled out of bed by the excitement to chase their dreams and help

others. That's why I believe we're at the highest rate of teen sui-
cides ever. We've got a whole lot of people doing a whole lot of
things they really don't want to do, at all.

To find meaning and purpose in life, you must create a direction, a vision, a dream—you must know what you want. But first,
you must stop telling yourself that dreams don't matter, that they
are only dreams and that you should be more sensible. Because
when you cease to dream and pursue your dreams, you cease to
live. So don't simply seek success, even if you want it. Instead, do
what you love and success will come. You only have one life and if
you're not doing what you love, what's the point of living it?

"What You Want" Exercise

I am going to ask you a question. I'd call it a million-dollar question, but that's pretty limited considering the possibilities that open
up when you know the answer. But before I ask, I want you to
know that I am going to ask in a few different ways, just in case
your response is, "I don't know. . . ." or "It doesn't matter. . . ." or
something else that avoids answering the question.

So here's the question:

What do you want?
What would have to happen in the next year for you to look back and say
that it was your most successful and fulfilling year yet?

Now, before we go on too much further, I know there are a lot
of people who'd say, "Hey! I don't know what I want! I just want to
fit in!" I know this because that's almost the only thing a lot of us
ever say in life about what we want—"I don't know." We don't
know what we want, so we just stand in line buying things that

other people want us to buy. We remain in a vicious cycle of not knowing what we want, yet not realizing that we don't know what we want because we're too distracted by what other people want us to want and by what we think we have to do.

I believe that life itself demands us to tell it what we want, because otherwise it's useless. Life is just waiting, asking, "How can I serve you?" But we don't know how it can serve us, and so we say, "I don't know. . . . It doesn't matter. . . . I don't matter. . . ." But if you didn't matter, you wouldn't be here.

Now, I'll ask again: *What would have to happen in the next year for you to look back and say it was your most successful and fulfilling year yet?*

Don't let your mind tell you that it can't be this easy! Allow it to be this easy. It is *that* easy. However, the problem is that what is easy to do is also easy to not do. And it sure would have been easy for a fourteen-year-old African-American kid to not stand up during one of my workshops and ask to make a statement.

I was in Portland, Oregon, speaking to a room full of mostly thirty-five- to sixty-year-olds, and I asked the same question, "What would have to happen in the next year for you to look back one year from now and say that it was your most successful and fulfilling year yet?" Just then, this little—it's hard to call him little with all the power he had in his heart—African-American boy stood up. He wanted to share: "I wanted to say that the answer to the question for me is that I want to write a book. The reason I want that is because it makes me feel like myself."

The room went silent. I began to feel threatened—perhaps this child could help my audience more than I could. He continued, "Everybody always wants me to be somebody, or something, or do something. And so, I think that we can find the answer to what we want by asking ourselves, 'What makes you feel like yourself?'"

It became so clear to everyone in the audience that we live in a world where everyone wants us to be something other than who we are. Where so often we become something other than ourselves, turning our life into a fight to get back to where we once were. I've been there too, and the solution is—just as this brilliant young adult advised—to do what makes you feel like yourself!

So what makes you feel like yourself? Play the *what-if* game, like when you were a kid. What if nothing could stop you? What if your answer couldn't be, "I don't know" or "There's too many things so I can't possibly choose. . . ."? What if you couldn't fail and your lack of resources couldn't limit you?

What would have to happen in the next year for you to look back and say that it was your most successful and fulfilling year yet? Take out a sheet of paper and define this in one or two sentences. Describe how your ideal life would look in one year. Don't think so much. Just feel.

The only way you can ever truly know something is by putting yourself there. To do so, you must time-travel (in your mind) to the future. Feel what it would be like to live this dream as though it were happening now. Get up and act it out if it helps you. Then, come back here and describe it. Did it feel wondrously beautiful? It should!

Writing down what you want is the first step to creating success and fulfillment. I received this exercise from Jack Canfield—one of the most successful men in the world of publishing and the creator of the Chicken Soup for the Soul book series.

Serious-less-ness

The world is like a ride in an amusement park. And when you choose to go on it you think it's real, because that's how

powerful our minds are . . . but don't worry, because this is
just a ride.

—Bill Hicks, American stand-up comedian,
social critic, satirist, and musician

Many people wish for life to be exclusively perfect. But the good
life that most desire is actually a life warmed by mistakes and hu-
mility. A life touched with a ceremonial grace, which is impossible
to live without occasionally picking your nose and dancing naked
(maybe not in public). And many people who seek perfection think
that life is like a math test—they think that if they don't get really
serious, they'll fail, or won't get straight A's. However, I think life
is more like those times when you think you misplaced your car
keys, but they are actually in your hand. We spend much of our
time intensely looking out into the world for life, but the keys to a
purpose-driven life are in our own hands, in our own perception.
As a result, we spend our time desperately trying to find life, when
it is actually already in our hands—we can choose how we wish to
live. So why not lighten up, be weird, and be yourself?

The mind is like a county fair. There are thousands of voices in
your head, all calling out to you to take their ride. They all tell you
what you must do, where and how you must look, and what you
should say. While at this fair, the majority of people tell you to buy
the ticket and take the ride. But have you ever wondered what
happens when you don't buy the ticket—if you choose not to do all
those things you think you must do in order for your life to be
perfect?

We spend a lot of our time trying to get everything just right,
stressing ourselves out, only to one day see that there was no need
to be so uptight. One of the things I know for sure is that a lot of
good things start to happen when you seriously get serious about

not being so serious. In fact, palliative nurse Bronnie Ware wrote a book, *The Top Five Regrets of the Dying: A Life Transformed by the Dearly Departing*, where she recorded her findings of common life regrets before death. One of the top reccurring regrets of her patients was, "I wish I would've let myself be happier. . . ."

Often we don't allow ourselves to be happier because we forget how close to death we truly are. We think that it's more important to look good or do well than it is to enjoy life. A man in one of my seminars perfectly illustrated this fact:

"Everyone stick your finger in your nose and smile!" I said, just before we took the picture at the end of the day.

One man, David, just couldn't do it. "This is ridiculous!" he said. "I can't do that!"

It had been a focused day, with a lot of hard work. We'd just finished and I wanted everybody to stop being so serious, to head home in a goofy mood so they wouldn't feel stressful about their goals. But this fifty-year-old man just couldn't do it. He thought he looked too stupid. Finally, the other thirty students in the room chanted his name until he caved in. His face went from bright red to gold and liberated.

It's funny how we spend our lives trying so hard and stressing so much, just to get it *right*. But the truth is no one knows what he or she is doing. Everything is just an idea. "Popular" and "cool" are just words we made up. And their definitions are attached to other ideas we made up about how you must dress and what you must do to be categorized by these labels. And later, the very ideas we created drive us crazy during our attempts to conform to them.

But conforming isn't worth it. Just take a look at some of the greatest contributors in the world: Steve Jobs, Albert Einstein, Jim Morrison, Ralph Waldo Emerson, Richard Branson—not only were they great influencers to the consciousness of humanity, but also they were (or still are) really, really weird. They didn't try to be normal—they were themselves and followed their wild imaginations. They didn't overly panic when they were in deep water all alone with no one by their side.

It reminds me of a story a friend once told me. He wasn't a good swimmer. In fact, he would describe himself as "aquahandicapped." One day he and his family and friends were on a boat off the coast of Catalina. They parked the boat off the dock. His kids decided to swim into shore. Shortly thereafter he had the urge to follow them in. It wasn't long until he was drowning. His arms flailed and he screamed, "Help me! Help me!" He yelled louder and louder, but all he heard was laughter from his kids. He could also see his friends laughing on the boat. Minutes passed and he was still screaming, but no one was coming. He was losing energy and began to sink. Suddenly, someone from a nearby boat jumped off and swam to him with a flotation device. Just before they got to him he sunk underwater, flailing violently, thinking he was about to die.

Moments later his head rose out of the water, followed by his shoulders, and eventually his chest. He was standing in chest-deep water with a smile on his face. He'd had the ability to stand the whole time. However, he was so panicked and caught up in the situation that he didn't realize this fact.

I think this is a perfect example of how most of us live our lives—believing that the water is deeper than it is—which results in our living in a constant state of worry, stress, and fear. We tense up our body, clench our teeth, sink our feet into the ground, and prepare for battle, which only further ensures that life turns into a never-ending war. We need to be less intense and learn to laugh at ourselves, because *the water just ain't that deep*!

We would enjoy life more if we'd just ask ourselves, "Is this situation going to be something that will determine how my life will be fifty years from now?" Usually the answer is no, despite the fact that we often believe that the answer is yes. We are tough on ourselves and forget that the moment we lighten up is the moment we become enlightened.

People often ask me, "How do I take life less seriously? How can I lower my stress?" The best place to start is by remembering that you're going to die soon. C'mon, just admit it. I remember the day I finally accepted that—my whole life changed. I was a freshman in college sitting on the beach under the sun. I sat there and thought, *This is all so great, and none of it's going to last. Why would I waste this precious time trying to be so serious?* I realized that I had no reason to do so, so that very day I stopped taking life so seriously.

You and me, our time is limited. Don't waste your time trying to make life so perfect that you do everything except live. Life is a thing far too important to take seriously. And a sense of humor is the main measure of sanity.

Taking Risks

Remember, a dead fish can float down a stream, but it takes a live one to swim upstream.

—W. C. Fields

Many of us have forgotten one of the wisest statements said in life, "If opportunity doesn't come, go get it." I am not sure if it was George Washington, Mike Tyson, Mother Teresa, or Charlie Sheen who originally said it, but I do know that it's something we all need to hear. Great opportunities are lost every day because the people who could have had them were afraid of being laughed at, failing, or stepping out of their comfort zone. The right moment is waiting for you to stop waiting for the right moment. Yet many of us never really experience our lives; we limit our existence because it feels comfortable. But just because you've been doing things a certain way for a while doesn't mean that it's the way you need to continue.

The world is built by those who take risks—pioneers who are not afraid of the unknown, businesspeople who are not afraid of failure, thinkers who are not afraid of progress, and dreamers who are not afraid of putting their dreams into action. Our cultural conditioning makes us believe that if we stay within our comfort zones, and avoid taking big risks, we are being safe, smart, and secure. I am going to let you in on a little secret—nothing is secure while you're alive. Not your job, your life, not even the existence of the human race. Even science can't explain important aspects of our existence, such as who we are and why we're here. We are flying on a rock through the middle of space and there's nothing else similar to our world out there (at least that we know of).

What makes you think that not risking what you have will make you smarter, safer, or more secure? It is especially important to consider this if you have a dream but are too scared to put it into action. What's more ill-advised than believing in your own excuses and living in fear your entire life? What's more dangerous than forgoing your desires because you think they are too risky? What's more dangerous than giving up on who you are and who you wish to be so that you can remain safe and comfortable?

Nothing.

Danger can never be overcome without taking risks. And if the purpose of your life is to live meaningfully, adventurously, and joyously, then how can you do it if you don't act on your desires, if you don't challenge yourself, if you don't seek adventure? Living life is risky. A bus *could* hit you while you cross the street later today. So does that mean that you should stay in your house for the rest of your life? *Probably not.* Chocolate could melt, spill onto your clothes, and ruin them. Should you fear that life might get dirty, and therefore wrap yourself in a plastic bag that covers you from head to toe? *Probably not.* Your morning coffee could be so hot that it burns your tongue. Should you therefore remove your tongue from your mouth as a precautionary measure? *Probably not.* You could spend your life working at a job you don't really love, but that pays well enough to give you a wonderful retirement (one day). But the economy could collapse or your business could fail, and you would end up having wasted years of your life. Alternatively, you could do what you love. Life is too short not to!

It's best to take big risks and do what you're afraid of, instead of doing what everyone (family, friends, society, etc.) wants you to do to be accepted and considered normal. Just because other people accept you doesn't mean you will accept yourself. The latter is only possible if you do what you love and not what you're supposed to do.

Happiness means living life on your own terms. It doesn't mean that everything is perfect and comfortable—it means that you've decided that the best way to live life is to take the leap and create it for yourself. The smartest thing you can do is the thing that you feel you should do, not the thing you think you're supposed to do. Yes, it's a risk to step into the unknown, to do something different, to follow your feelings, to make a change, to face your fears, to try something new that you may fail at; but that is where the joy of life comes from—the thrill of uncertainty.

Unfortunately, we tend to make decisions by asking ourselves, "What's the worst that can happen?" Then, we imagine all the possible outcomes (or disasters) in our heads. We see the scenario where we try something new, and fail. Or where someone gets mad at us, where we lose our jobs, where we get embarrassed, where someone says no, and so on and so forth. We tend to only focus on the negative things that can happen. We are afraid that if all goes wrong, all will really suck. And thinking this way makes it so that we never try.

That's why most of us live long lives with spirits that are already dead by the time we finish college. We try too hard to fit in, be smart, safe, and comfortable. Instead of choosing this route, consider asking yourself, **"What's the *best* that can happen if I *finally* do this?"** It's the very possibility of failure that prevents us from trying. That's why asking the above question is so important.

Have we forgotten that Thomas Edison failed miserably literally thousands of times before creating the light bulb? Or that Steve Jobs was fired from Apple—the very company he created? Or that Michael Jordan missed hundreds of game-winning shots— letting his team down? Or that Jack Canfield, creator of Chicken Soup for the Soul (one of the bestselling book series in publishing history), was denied by 144 publishing companies before he finally got a "yes" to publish the first book?

We seem to forget that Oprah was fired from her first job in entertainment and told that she had no future in the industry. How surfer Laird Hamilton (who at one time surfed the largest wave in world history) risked dying to ride giant waves that ultimately inspired tens of millions of people worldwide to conquer their fears. In fact, one time I interviewed him about risks and fear, and he told me, "Life is about doing what can't be done. If more people knew that, they would achieve the impossible, and risk everything to get there."

We must remember that every great artist, athlete, writer, musician, and business mogul was none of these things before their monumental achievements. They simply took the risk to get there. All the people who our society looks up to (and most people who you probably personally look up to) risked all that was safe, secure, and comfortable to get what they really wanted out of life.

Since the dawn of humankind, our heroes have shown us that risk-taking is the key to all great achievements and contributions to humanity—it's an ability that every purpose-driven, highly effective, successful, and fulfilled person has. The people we honor in our media and textbooks, those who inspire us, are those who have walked away from what is secure and normal—from fads, trends, and fears, as well as from the fleeting illusion of "comfortability." They have carved a place in history because of this choice. Courage and risk-taking are what allow people to take action in spite of what could go wrong.

Stories of courageous individuals demonstrate that it's crazy if there's something you love to do and aren't doing it, or if you have a gift and aren't using it (for whatever reason). In fact, it's by far the most dangerous choice. You're suffocating your desires, your spirit, your joy, and your passions. You're compromising your purpose in life if you don't take the leap and do what you love. And it doesn't matter how much or how little you've achieved in your life—there's always room to take that next step.

You're only going to have the body you have now once—just one time. And you're only going to have the opportunities that come to you each day once as well. Tomorrow brings different opportunities and challenges. You have just one life! You're only going to have the urges, impulses, and desires that make up who you are in this lifetime one time. And if you don't act on them, they will bottle up inside of you as regrets that fill your mind on your deathbed. The opportunities to follow your heart—as it may guide you toward many things—are once in a lifetime. If the universe sees that you are unwilling to trust it, unwilling to give up the choking monotony of ordinary existence for something far larger and more enlivening, it will spend its time investing its energy in someone else who is willing to risk it all in order to have it all. And by having it all, I don't mean having every possession known to mankind. I mean having the inner fulfillment of knowing that you are living life on your own terms. Of finding a sense of adventure and excitement that comes with the territory of stepping out of the boundaries of what you believe is possible for your life. This is the thrill and benefit of having "risk-ability."

Are you on a course for a promising and secure future, yet it isn't the future you really dream of? Steve Jobs found himself in the same predicament at one time, and yet he is one of the greatest contributors to the twenty-first century. So how did he do it? He risked everything. By dropping out of college he risked what most would consider a very promising future, but he did so because he wasn't doing what he loved. He felt that doing something he wasn't absolutely passionate about was a waste of time. He believed that the biggest risk was wasting your life—settling by not doing what you love. So he took risks that most would be afraid to take. He quit school and started sleeping on the floor of his friends' dorm rooms. He was so broke that he had to collect bottles to exchange them for money so that he could feed himself. But it didn't matter— he was on a journey to uncover meaning in his life, rather than simply do what others told him was safe, secure, and smart.

Spending your days doing anything less than what you dream of is not worth it. And the only way to start is by taking that first step—it's impossible to control everything and have a perfect plan before you begin; it doesn't work that way. You just need to begin. And if you pursue what you love to do with all of your being, *the way* will be made for you. Additionally, your confidence will build along the way because you will start to do that which scares you and you'll overcome your fears. Purpose is not a matter of chance, but a matter of choice—you do not wait for it, but find it through action. Are you placing enough freakish, interesting, long-shot, weirdo bets to quench your desire for excitement?

If you believe that the best decision for the rest of your life is whatever is easiest and most normal, then what you have to lose is life itself. Remember, if you cling to comfort and conformity, and are afraid to do what you know you must, you will never be free. How can liberation, meaning, and joy come from knowing what's going to happen each and every day? It can't!

Do you think the fabulously successful actor Brad Pitt knew what was going to happen to his life when he decided to drop out of college? He bravely did so two weeks before graduation, moving from Missouri to Southern California to pursue his passion for acting. Do you think that this was a smooth, easy change that made it peaceful and simple for him to build his extraordinary legacy? If you do, then maybe you should know that when Brad moved to Los Angeles, he was so broke that he took a job as a mascot for a fast food company. He was challenged so much that he had to wear a chicken costume to pay his bills and pursue his dreams. And moving to Los Angeles was not his only choice; he had left behind a much more secure lifestyle. He took a risk because he knew that if you risk nothing, you risk everything. He knew that taking heart-guided risks leads to living a meaningful life and gives you opportunities to live for something greater than your own comfort and security—for adventure, for meaning, for thrill, and for purpose.

Another great example is Jackie Robinson, the African-American Hall of Fame baseball player, who risked his own life to do what he loved and, in doing so, gave the opportunity to play ball to millions of African-Americans around the world. He altered not only professional sports history, but also human history. Do you think it wasn't a risk to muster up the courage and head out to the batter's box during the height of racism in America? Everyone in the stadium (including the opposing coach) was yelling a slew of racial slurs, which included threats against Jackie's life. Choosing to have his existence threatened by doing what he loved and what he felt he deserved to do with his life was a risky choice. But Jackie Robinson walked out to that batter's box regardless of the risks— and by being courageous he made it possible for black people to play professional baseball.

Big results such as the one mentioned above are what is possible when you take risks. You influence the lives of countless people and inspire an endless number of individuals. And all of this is possible because by following your heart you prove that you can get more out of life than the "same stuff, different day" response that many people give when you ask them how life is treating them. The more you risk, the more opportunities you have for excitement and reward.

About now is when many people start asking, "What if the results are a little less than ideal and I get my heart and mind torn apart?" Or, "What if I fail and feel humiliated, scared, and uncertain?" If your dream does not come true, I suggest that you get back up and try again (of course, only if your objective is to experience life and find more meaning). It doesn't mean that your dream can't shift and change as you go along. You will know what to do as long as you keep following your heart—it will lead you down the right path. And following your heart means following your joy. It's the joyful being that begs for an occasional fright, a jolt from normality, a dance on the floor of life—their own little festival of craziness and impossibility. When you do this you'll see

that it wasn't so improbable (and isn't so scary) to veer off the pre-
scribed path.

Process over Outcomes

A self-actualized person is one who is focused on the process
of their work rather than the outcome, results, or setbacks.

—Abraham Maslow, American psychologist

Imagine that you're a high-profile athlete in one of the most
media-centered and lucrative industries in the world. You've been
sponsored by some of the world's largest companies, and have won
some of the biggest competitions in your sport. Also, you're making more money than you know what to do with. Then, one day,
you decide you've had enough. You leave the limelight at the pinnacle of your career. The judges, companies, media, fans, and your
competition watch your exit while scratching their heads. . . .

Your decision came one day while reflecting on why you
started following your dream in the first place. You remember that
the thrill was in doing, in getting lost in the process, and in the
journey toward focusing wholeheartedly on the thing you love.
Getting lost in your passion is what gave your life meaning, not
whether or not you were successful in everyone else's eyes. However, it became impossible to escape those eyes while cameras were
following you everywhere—while people were more focused on
your competition rankings than your enjoyment and your trials
and triumphs as a person. You realize that you've been reduced
to being considered a number in a ranking system, which is ironic
because when you originally chose this path it was in part to avoid
becoming just another number. You didn't follow your bliss to be

the best or to win the most awards, but to be happy. So, as a result of this reflection, you leave it all behind and live in a tent on the outskirts of civilization in Indonesia for a year.

This is actually not a fictional story. It is the story of Rob Machado, whom many regard as one of surfing's most important legends. In a world where many of us are focused on how we can get more attention, material objects, rewards, money, and fame, Rob surprised us by wanting something different—more meaning.

Machado recalled his decision to quit competing while we sat on his couch. I listened to him attentively. "I had two offers on the table at this point. One had the potential to be very lucrative, but it was completely based off of touring, competing, and winning. I would have to win this, and do this and that. Then, on the other hand, I had a contract offer from Hurley. They had a different approach. They said, 'We like you. You're cool. We want you to do what you love and have fun. Enjoy the process and forget the outcomes. . . .' So I picked Hurley's contract. It was less money, but it was a no-brainer."

He could have said to himself, "Ah, man, well, I need to be in the spotlight and make lots of money, so I'll do what I need to do to ensure that I stay here. I guess this is what it takes to be in this industry and be a star." But he didn't. Instead he chose to say, "I came here to do what I love, to have fun, to help others, and to find meaning in life, so I'll do whatever I need to do to make that my priority." And he meant it.

Humanity would have drastically different stories to tell if more frequently we adopted the process of finding meaning in life, rather than solely focusing on results, and ego-driven benefits. If, instead, our purpose was to live life as a journey toward doing what we love and what fulfills us each day, we wouldn't be at the highest rate of depression per capita that we've seen in human history. However, instead of realizing this, and following the pure essence of our dreams, many of us judge choices such as Rob's. Many ask, "Why would anyone give up fame? Why would anyone leave so much money on the table?"

While sitting silently and listening to Rob's story on his couch, I was reminded of the work of Abraham Maslow, one of my favorite thinkers. Maslow coined a phrase for what he considers the world's most highly functioning individuals. He called them *self-actualizers*. A quality that separates a highly functioning person from the rest is that they are focused on the *process*, rather than the outcome. They do what they do because they love to do it. Their focus is not on what they'll get as a result (such as success and stardom), but on how they can get lost in the journey of their passion.

Rob felt that there was more to life than trophies and achievements. He knew that these things only brought a peak of excitement that would eventually fade away. If you define yourself solely by your achievements, then you won't find yourself, because as soon as you think you know who you are, that peak is gone (and perhaps it's even being enjoyed by someone else). So you end up back to where you once were, left wondering who you are. To know yourself, to be a self-actualizing person, you must focus on creating. Don't let outcomes and results control your life. Spend your energy doing what you do best. The rest are details that will try to distract you from your true joy in life.

Unfortunately, however, all too often we hear about the scenario opposite from Rob's. We hear about celebrities losing all they have, even their health and happiness, just to achieve outcomes. They strive to be better than everyone else and make the most money. They become overly distracted by the results their passion created, and lose interest in the passion itself.

When we're overly invested in results, achievements, and expectations, pressure is created, which blocks us from feeling meaning. Purpose, in its true form, is when you're open to the spontaneity of what your passion brings to your life, as opposed to requiring a specific outcome to feel contentment. Don't get me wrong, it's absolutely important to have a vision (I stressed this a lot earlier in this chapter), but it's also important to remember that meaning comes while on the path toward that vision, not once you achieve it. Therefore, contentment, at least for those who want to be highly functioning people, comes from our process rather than our outcomes—we are aware that fame, money, and approval are consequences of our process that are always short-lived. We are put in a powerful state of alignment with our purpose when we engage in our work for the pleasure of the process, rather than waiting for the end results.

I can recall when I thought that publishing my first book was going to fulfill me. I had a blast writing the book—I truly enjoyed every moment. However, I always thought that the *really* amazing feeling would come when I got the book published. And finally that day came. I remember taking a screenshot of the travel section rankings of my book on Amazon.com. It was one ahead of one of my favorite books, *Into the Wild*, and one behind an acclaimed best seller, *Eat, Pray, Love*. I was in pure bliss. I just looked at it for the whole night. *Wow*, I thought, *aren't I awesome?*

However, that feeling didn't last too long. The next day I had three back-to-back speaking engagements, and I didn't have time to think about outcomes because I had to stay in the process of sharing my story. I remember lying down on my hotel bed that night thinking, *Was that it? Was that seriously how short-lived the pride of my achievement was?*

Up until that point my focus had been on two things: creating new writing material and inspiring people through speeches. And that day it had switched to my success, to thoughts such as, *How awesome am I? I am right behind* Eat, Pray, Love*!* That night I realized that positive results are great and achieving goals is fun, but they are simply a means to an end, and they can distract us from what got us there in the first place—doing what we love and sharing that gift with others.

Achievements, good results, and positive outcomes are great indicators that we're doing well. But that's all they can ever be. They aren't the source of happiness because they are external things. Happiness comes from the internal process of loving what you do. And that night I also realized that if I wanted to live a purpose-driven life, like Rob's, then I couldn't measure who I was based on external circumstances and rankings. From now on I needed to gauge myself based on whether or not I was connected to what I love doing. I needed to ensure that I was spending my time doing what I love and wasn't letting result-oriented goals distract me from my true joy.

Getting caught up on seeking specific outcomes directs our focus away from our true intentions, which are usually to have fun and make a difference. I wrote a book because I wanted to inspire people. Yet I got so caught up in rankings that it became more about being on top than it was about inspiring people and staying true to my mission. If we contradict our own values and principles, what are we left with? Nothing.

We've all heard of Sylvester Stallone, the screenwriter and main actor of the Oscar-winning, legendary movie *Rocky*. However, most of us only know his story from the time he was successful and doing well, when the truth is that things weren't always easy for him. His dream was to inspire people by writing scripts and acting in them. He had the drive and the courage to write many scripts—the only problem, though, was that he couldn't sell any of them. He was so broke that his wife threatened to leave him

if he didn't look for another job. But Sylvester didn't give up because he was too in love with the process of his work. It's what
made him feel alive. He couldn't quit simply because he had not
yet achieved positive results. He couldn't compromise his dreams.

Eventually, his wife left him. At that point he was so broke
that all he had left was his dog, and he didn't have enough money
for either of them to eat. That day he headed down to the local li-
quor store and sold his dog for fifty bucks. Sylvester said it was the
worst day of his life. But he didn't focus on the lack of positive
results and pain of losing his four-footed friend. Instead, he knew
that this sacrifice meant that he truly needed to continue to do
what he loved as best as he could.

Not long after, Sylvester got the inspiration for the screenplay
Rocky and wrote the script in twenty-four hours. He knew it was
going to be huge. His dream was to make it a major motion picture, and act in it too. He felt that this would be a journey that
would give him meaning and purpose. And it wasn't long after he
finished the script that he was offered $100,000 for it from a major
film production company.

Try to imagine this scenario for a minute: You're a broke
writer and actor, your wife just left you, you have no money, you
had to sell your dog so that you could eat, and yet you continue to
follow your dreams in spite of the fact that you have yet to achieve
positive results. And then, finally, you're offered $100,000 (which
at the time was far more money than it is today) for your script.
But there is one issue—you are given a condition from the film
company in the buying of the script—not only will you not be the
leading actor in the film, but you won't be acting in the film at all.
What would you do?

If there's one thing that most people who've lived their dreams
have in common, it's that they don't compromise when it comes to

their dreams. Even if they keep getting told "no," or life presents them with circumstances different from what their original vision was, they just don't give up. They are in the process of doing what they love, and see only that journey. Therefore, regardless of the outcome, they aren't swayed from what they want and love. It should come as no surprise, then, that Sylvester declined the offer.

The next week they came again and offered him $200,000. Sylvester asked, "Am I Rocky?" They told him no. He declined again, and again, and again. Until they offered him $1,000,000, thinking that surely this broke artist would take that outcome, right? But he didn't.

The following week they called again and offered him $50,000 and the lead role. He jumped at the opportunity and accepted it with the utmost excitement. It wasn't long after that he won two Oscars (including one for best actor in a leading role), and the rest is history. He chose to stay consumed in the process and journey of his vision, of doing what he loved, and didn't let the outside world, outcomes, or circumstances push him off the path of what he loved most.

Consider that you're no different from Sylvester Stallone or Rob Machado—that you too have a passionate drive that gets you up each day. That you also deserve to be on the journey of what brings you the most joy. And imagine that the only way you will fail to keep doing what you love and living your joy is by giving more power to the outside world, to the outcomes (or lack thereof), than to your inner world—than to your own happiness. The process of overcoming the hurdles of life, and not compromising on your passion, is what gives your life meaning.

Chapter 2

What's Your "Why"?

Get off the field, or we'll kill you, fucking nigger!

—ANONYMOUS PERSON YELLING
AT JACKIE ROBINSON

That wasn't the first time he'd heard it—hearing racial remarks was an everyday occurrence while Jackie Robinson was breaking the color barrier in Major League Baseball (against the wishes of most of America). Robinson couldn't have been the first African-American to play Major League Baseball had he not known what he was fighting for—equal rights for American citizens. With a goal like that, he had a tremendous source of motivation to draw upon—it was larger than he was, larger than life. As a result, he altered the history of America.

Rules are often restrictions and criticism usually impedes our progress, because we long to be accepted, not rejected. So how could Jackie Robinson keep going when he was violently rejected, relentlessly threatened, and constantly uncomfortable? Because he knew that what he wanted was more important than what life had been offering him. He knew *why* he wanted to do what he was doing, and even if only a tiny portion of the global population accepted his desires, a pure, pulsing, selfless reason can never be silenced.

Jackie Robinson bettered the lives of countless people because he believed that "a life is not important except in the impact it has on other lives." This view made it easy for him to have motivation and fuel. What would you do if you believed that life was meaningless unless it impacted people's lives?

It's no mystery, then, that when Jackie saw an opportunity to impact lives forever, he didn't give up. How could he give up on such a large driving force? He couldn't . . . and that is how he changed the world.

Reason Creates Emotion, Emotion Controls Action, Action Creates Direction, and Direction Dictates Life

At the very least, most people have an idea of what they want, even if they never get it. There are many causes for failing to get what we want. Perhaps the most significant and overlooked reason for not getting what we want is not knowing why we are doing what we're doing in the first place.

It's pretty hard to do anything if nothing is driving you. The mind has the potential to bring you almost any feeling, including energy and drive. But the mind can't do this if it doesn't know why it's doing it. If you don't have strong driving forces that pull you out of bed when you're tired, keep you up when you want to go to bed, or inspire you to take action when you want to call it quits, then your mind has no fuel to create what you want, even if you know you want it.

You're destined to either feel lazy and tired, or get busy. That's why you need reasons to motivate you when you don't feel like doing much. Similarly, just because you know how you want your life to go doesn't mean that it will go that way. In fact, most of the time it probably won't. And often, when this happens, people give up. People don't take action on their dreams, talk to people they find attractive, or keep going toward a goal because they are un-comfortable and don't want to risk criticism. This is why we need reasons to do things that keep us motivated. Why get out of bed early if there's no reason to do so? I know I can't.

Your mind and body can create or do almost anything if they know why they must do it. Life's circumstances are malleable, and based on the emotions from which you are living. Mothers can pick up school buses to save their children in the name of love.

If inspiring reasons get us up each day, they create excitement, confidence, and appreciation in our lives. If you know why you want something, you're going to be more focused. Knowing *why* gives you a psychological incentive to make it happen.

If we're just carrying on throughout the day because we don't know what else to do, it breeds fear, stress, and worry. We believe that we are subject to whatever life throws at us. Living under these circumstances is like living inside an iron cage that we've created with the belief that we cannot shape life how we want it. If we know why we want something (or to live in a certain way), we can draw upon our passion to overcome any obstacles to get-ting it.

"Finding Your Motivation" Exercise

Why do you wake up in the morning? Why do you put clothes on and go through your day? Why do you work where you work? Why do you live how you live? Why are you the way you are? Why do you work on your talents? Why do you have a dream? Why do you want to do what you love?

There are a lot of people who aren't successful and happy in life because they don't have anything motivating them. You need something that can make you say no to the snooze button, something that makes you want to get up earlier each day. You need something that propels you to move forward even when you are criticized. You need to write down your "why." And if your "why" in life is to be famous or to make a lot of money, take this a step further and think about what you would do when you receive that money and after everyone knows who you are. And yes, after buying that car and that amazing house . . . what comes after that? What would be your next step? Why would you be doing what you are doing?

One of the World's Greatest

"He's great because he knows why he's getting out on the court every night," Eric Thomas, the motivational speaker, stated. He was talking about NBA all-star and Olympic athlete Kevin Durant. Durant is one of the world's best basketball players, and is also one of its most focused and quietest. He doesn't show off after he scores, he doesn't get into arguments with the other team, and he doesn't dance when he dunks. He just plays the game as best as he can, every night.

Eric explained that the first thing that Durant does when he steps on the court before each game is touch the front and back number on his jersey. He wears the number 35. "Why does he touch it?" Thomas asked rhetorically. "He does it for the coach that he feels helped make him who he is today." Durant's coach was killed at thirty-five years old, thus the significance of his number. Durant plays for his coach. He wants to win an NBA championship for him. When Durant plays he sees the big picture, and that is why he is one of the most composed athletes in the world—he knows why he does what he does. This gives him strength so that he does not fret about losing a game, or about having a bad shooting game, or about making a big dunk—these are not his big goals because he is playing for something more than that. And the thing that motivates him keeps him composed, disciplined, and focused.

Overcoming Situations through Powerful Motives

> Get up every morning and ask: "Am I doing the things that I believe in and am I doing them for the best possible motives?"
>
> —Nick Clegg

Life tests your character. Each event in your life gives you an opportunity to see how you'll react and who you are. Your current life situation doesn't have to be your future, but it will be if you don't make any changes.

Sadly, most of us live life without a genuine motive behind our work and our day-to-day activities. Having reasons for why you do what you do doesn't mean that you won't feel pain, but it will help keep you going strong when you want to give up. Many of us say, "If only . . ." or "But this keeps happening, so I can't because . . ." or "Every time I try, life has other plans. So what's the use?"

When we say these things to ourselves, or to others, we are implying (unconsciously, of course) that we don't have the power to change things. We act as though Gandhi was some superhuman, isolated phenomenon. When his countrymen were being oppressed by British rule he could've said, "Oh, what's the use? We keep losing our freedom and that's the way it is. The British are stronger and they have more resources."

But instead he said, "You must be the change you wish to see in the world," and "Life has no value unless I help others." He was sick of seeing his people suffer. He wanted to make a change that allowed people to live more freely. He had a clear objective, desire, and reasoning behind what he was doing. He wanted to stop oppression, which drove him to achieve what had previously seemed impossible.

Gandhi is known to have said, "A small body of determined spirits fired by an unquenchable faith in their mission can alter the course of history." He didn't believe in giving up. Giving up would imply that circumstance determines destiny, but this isn't true. Destiny is found in how determined you are to alter life—to take failure and rejection and, in spite of it, continue to believe that you can create something greater. Still, thinking this way can only get you so far. It is still essential that you know why you do what you do. If you are driven to do something for the right reasons, you can do the most incredible things.

The "Why" Exercise

Write down ten reasons *why* you want to live the way you've imagined. Underline the most powerful reason. Let it all soak in—feel that excitement and use it to propel you forward! Refer to this list whenever you need motivation and strength—keep rereading it. This is an important exercise because when you come to roadblocks or challenges while reaching your goals, you will feel much more inspired by looking at this list. It is a much better motivator than simply saying, "I am doing this because I have to," or "I don't know why I'm doing this."

1.

2.

3.

4.

5.

6.

7.

8.

9.

10.

Chapter 3

Failure and Courage

Anything is possible if you have enough nerve.

—J. K. ROWLING, BRITISH NOVELIST BEST KNOWN
AS THE AUTHOR OF THE HARRY POTTER SERIES

J. K. Rowling, author of the Harry Potter series and one of the most successful authors of the twenty-first century, traveled a road to success that was laced with pain and poverty. Rowling once lived on state benefits while dealing with the death of her mother after a divorce from her husband, yet she is now a billionaire who touches the lives of hundreds of millions of people.

Seven years after graduating from university, Rowling regarded herself as "the biggest failure" she knew. Her marriage had failed, she had a child to take care of, and she was without a job. If you were in her shoes, what would you think about your situation? She had an interesting way of describing it: ". . . [F]ailure meant a stripping away of the inessential. I stopped pretending to myself that I was anything other than what I was, and began to direct all my energy to finishing the only work that mattered to me. . . . I was set free, because my greatest fear had been realized, and I was still alive, and I still had a daughter whom I adored, and I had an old typewriter, and a big idea. And so rock bottom became a solid foundation on which I rebuilt my life."

Seeing beauty, even during the darkest hours, is one of the most incredible abilities that humans have. Rowling took time to reflect on her life, and saw where she could improve. She knew that she needed to be herself in order to succeed—her inability to be her authentic self was one of the main reasons she was failing. The seed for the success we desire often lies in the very place we are failing.

Rowling is a perfect example of the fact that anything is possible, especially if you don't accept the circumstances of your failures. We must remember that our failures come to teach us something. Rowling realized that she could succeed if she directed all of her energy toward what she loved most. Most people direct their energy in too many directions, and extend themselves too far in roles that don't fit them best. However, Rowling did just the opposite—she believed in her idea, went for it, and made it her priority.

Fear of Failure Doesn't Need to Stop You

Oprah Winfrey is another perfect example that fear and failure don't have to lead to your defeat. We hear so much about Oprah's success—the lives she's touched and the billions of dollars she has made following her passion. But none of it would've been possible if she let failure decide her fate, if she didn't see failure as nothing more than a stepping-stone to greater heights.

Before her success, Oprah was demoted from her co-anchor news position because "she wasn't fit for television." Isn't that hilarious, after all that she has accomplished on television? Not only does she have her own show, but she's ended up having her own network! Unfortunately, physical appearance is often something that keeps us from trying things in the first place, but Oprah's image didn't stop her. Instead she told herself, "Do the one thing you think you cannot do. Fail at it. Try again. Do better the second time. The only people who never tumble are those who never mount the high wire. This is your moment. Own it."

I would be willing to bet that Oprah still felt fearful and insecure, but she didn't let that stop her—she knew what she wanted and I'm sure she also knew why she wanted it. For Oprah, failing was just another chance to try again and better her skills. Yet, somehow, most of us believe that failure means that we aren't good enough and should stop trying. But failure *isn't* a sign to stop—rather, it is a sign to keep going.

Big Waves Equals Big Courage

I learned that courage was not the absence of fear, but the triumph over it.

—Nelson Mandela, South African antiapartheid
revolutionary, politician, and philanthropist

I interviewed Laird Hamilton, legendary big-wave surfer and co-inventor of tow-in surfing, who told me that "fear of failure does one of two things—it paralyzes you, or it makes you stronger." Laird explained that when you feel fear you can either stop putting yourself out there or you can use that fear to get you back up and keep you going. He explained that he was always scared when the waves he rode were big enough to kill him, but because he knew what he wanted, he used that fear to make himself work harder. So it's always a choice—to try, or not to try. It's inevitable that you will feel the fear of failure, but it's optional to let that defeat you.

While I interviewed Hamilton, I learned that life gave him every reason not to be where he is today. And where is that? Especially on the faces of 100-foot waves that he surfed. You may or may not know who Laird is, but if you search for a video of him on YouTube, I am confident that you'll be amazed by his ability to ride the giant faces of waves that would kill just about anyone else.

I had Hamilton write the foreword to my first book because I felt he had it all—two happy children, a successful marriage with his wife, good looks, a paycheck bigger than he could spend earned from doing what he loved most, and a healthy body and mind. But what I didn't know before interviewing him was that, before his success, he actually had every reason to throw in the towel and say, "Aw, well, what's the use?"

Hamilton grew up in a tin shack without running water in Hawaii. He did not have a father and was relentlessly picked on because he was one of the few white people who lived where he grew up. He had no money, and no way to get a surfboard. However, he didn't let his circumstances and lack of resources determine what he could do with his life—Hamilton wanted to surf. One day he sat on a beach called Pipeline and waited until a surfer broke his board and threw it in the trash. Laird ran over to the trash, grabbed the front end of the snapped board, and began learning to surf on a broken piece of wood.

This was the first time that I had ever heard this story and I was shocked. "Again, Jake," Hamilton continued, "no matter how bad your life is, someone has got it worse. You can cry, 'poor little old me,' and live your whole life believing that you don't deserve better, or you can decide to change what is happening and create a better life." And that's exactly what Hamilton did—even with his humble beginnings of learning to surf with a broken board, he dared to dream of surfing the biggest waves in the world.

It was not an easy path. Everyone Hamilton knew told him that he shouldn't try to accomplish his dream. Even his grade-school teachers told him that he could never do it, that he wouldn't make any money, and that he needed to think about that because he couldn't survive by eating his surfboard. "You can live your life listening to other people or listening to yourself," Hamilton told me. When we listen to ourselves, all the stories we make up about why something is impossible fade away. We become unreasonable and we create what we want out of life.

Becoming Unreasonable

George Bernard Shaw said, "The reasonable man adapts himself to the world. The unreasonable one persists in trying to adapt the world to himself. Therefore all progress depends on the unreasonable man." It took me a few times to read through this quote before I truly understood what Shaw was saying. My interpretation is that the more you rationalize and create reasons for why life is the way it is, the more likely you are to find reasons why you can't do what you want to do and, as a result, you psych yourself out.

People who live life on their own terms are those who don't accept the world's terms as fact. The people who reach their goals and live their dreams are the ones who, thinking logically, have every reason not to, and who have the most barriers in their way. The people who get the most out of themselves and life are those who have found ways to achieve what they wanted to achieve despite hardship.

If tapping into your ultimate potential is important to you, then sooner or later you need to realize that your willpower is stronger than the power of your willingness to believe that you're powerless. If you want to live a certain way, then live that way! Don't wait for life to make it so, because that may never happen. Make it so yourself by being unreasonable—by having no logical explanation for how something is possible other than the fact that you want it so badly and that it's so important to you and to those around you. Believe that you can do it, no matter what.

Failure Isn't Permanent

The brick walls are there for a reason. The brick walls are not there to keep us out. The brick walls are there to give us a chance to show how badly we want something. The brick walls are there to stop the people who don't want it badly enough. They're there to stop the *other* people.

—Randy Pausch, professor of computer science, human-computer interaction, and design at Carnegie Mellon University, and a bestselling author, who also achieved fame for his speech "The Last Lecture" at Carnegie Mellon University, after being diagnosed with pancreatic cancer with only a few months to live

Have you noticed that all of the greatest athletes have failed? Michael Jordan was cut from his high school basketball team, yet he became one of the greatest professional players in the world. And even so, he missed twenty-six game-winning shots during his career. He once said, "I have missed over nine thousand shots in my career. I have lost almost three hundred games. On twenty-six occasions I have been entrusted to take the game-winning shot, and I have missed. I have failed over and over and over again in my life. And that is why I succeed." For it is not failure that stops most people, but rather the belief that failure is permanent. Failure is nothing more than a storm in the weather forecast for the week—it comes and it goes, and it waters next season's yield because it teaches us where we can improve.

Use success and failure as indicators of your state of mind—are you feeling like you want to give up or adjust? The highly effective person knows that both success and failure are temporary, that there is much to learn from both. They know that one success or failure should never stop them from their primary focus, which is to continue to grow.

Michael Jordan also said, "I can accept failure, everyone fails at something. But I can't accept not trying." We tend to forget that everyone fails. Which means that what is much worse than failing is not trying. You must continuously challenge yourself—it will bring you much more happiness than if you choose to never allow yourself to fail because you've played it safe your whole life. Don't be so concerned about whether or not you've failed, but about whether or not you're content with your failure. And by content, I don't mean that you're thrilled by failure, but that you're comfortable with having only tried once.

Reject Rejection

You have losses that you never thought you'd experience. You have rejection and you have to learn how to deal with that and how to get up the next day and go on with it.

—Taylor Swift, Grammy-winning American country
music singer-songwriter

American business magnate Walt Disney was fired from a newspaper for "lacking imagination" and having "no original ideas." However, he used this failure to strengthen what he loved most—imagination and ideas. He did not take getting fired personally. He recognized that failure is an event, not a person—failure wasn't who he was, regardless of what anyone thought of him. What failed was the circumstance he was in.

Another great example of failure is the music group the Beatles. They were rejected by Decca Recording Studios, whose reason for not signing them was, "We don't like their sound. They have no future in show business." And, in spite of these remarks, they had a future so bright that it impacted the lives of young people around the world and changed music forever.

Albert Einstein could also be considered a failure. He didn't even speak until he was four or read till he was seven. His teachers believed that he would never amount to anything. In fact, at one point he was even expelled from school and denied admission to the Zurich Polytechnic School. But failure didn't stop him from following his heart, and he developed the theory of relativity, among many other things, which influenced the way we perceive and understand the way the world works.

By looking at these examples, we see that some of the people we look up to the most have failed (and often more than once). So, could the true definition of failing be not sticking to the purpose that you see as best for yourself, regardless of what happens and what others think? I believe so. You always have the option to see defeat as temporary or permanent—you get to choose with your attitude and perspective. A negative situation or viewpoint can only bring you down if *you* let it.

You need to be conscious about the way you interpret what others may call *fact*. In order to check if something is true for you, ask yourself, "Is this true, or is it just someone's opinion? Is this where I am choosing to be defeated, or is it only the beginning? Can I (and do I) want to start again? Or have I arrived at the end, where I want to stay? Am I being punished? Or am I simply learning and being prepared for something more? Is this what I'm willing to settle for, or do I want something more? Have I given it all my effort?"

Disregard what others say or what the fearful voice in your head says. Listen to your heart, and if it continues to tell you that you are on the right path, then ignore the fact that things are not working out as quickly and as easily as you had hoped. Nothing is permanent unless you allow it to be. We can't avoid failing. And besides, succeeding may feel great, but if you're really going to do something with your life, then the secret is learning how to fail gracefully. No one gets through life without feeling defeated at some time or another. If you can get back up after being knocked down, and stay persistent until you succeed, you'll eventually arrive where you were trying to go.

More Global Greats Who Failed or Faced Major Challenges

There are many examples of people who have made it to their goal despite setbacks, failures, and challenges that have come in their way. I have chosen to recap seven more people's stories, all of which have really inspired me. I hope that these people's stories give you the courage to overcome whatever it is that you are afraid of or that you think is holding you back.

Bethany Hamilton: World Champion Female Surfer
Whose Whole Arm Was Bitten off by a Shark

Hamilton entered her first surf competition when she was only eight years old and truly loved the sport. However, at age thirteen, a shark attacked her and she lost her left arm. In spite of the horror and fear that she must have felt after what had happened to her, she was back on her surfboard one month later, and, two years after that, she won first place in the Explorer Women's Division of the 2005 NSSA National Championships. She continued to do what she loved regardless of her new physical setback. She may be one of the best female surfers in the world, but what is even more special and inspiring than that is her determination to keep going despite her difficult situation. And as a result, Bethany has shared her inspirational message of hope and courage with millions of people, and her story has been made into an inspiring major motion picture called *Soul Surfer.*

Steven Spielberg Was Rejected from University of
Southern California (USC), Twice (and Some Say
It Was Actually Three Times)

Yes, one of the most prolific filmmakers of all time, the man who brought us movies like *Jaws*, *E.T.*, and *Jurassic Park*, failed to get into USC, which was the film school of his choice. In the end, Spielberg got the last laugh and USC awarded him an honorary degree in 1994. Two years later, he became a trustee of the university.

Anthony Robles: Champion Wrestler with One Leg

Robles began his career on the mat in his high school. He said that his first match as a small, ninety-pound freshman did not go well. But this didn't stop him from trying, and he kept improving each time he went out on the mat. In March 2011, the all-American Arizona State University student won the NCAA championship title for the 125-pound weight class division. What I love most about him is that he said, "I didn't get into the sport for the attention. I wrestle because I love wrestling. . . . But if I can help change somebody's life for the better, then that's an honor."

Elvis Presley the Truck Driver?

After a performance at Nashville's Grand Ole Opry, the concert hall manager told Elvis that he was better off returning to Memphis and driving trucks (his former career) than continuing his singing career. Thank God he didn't listen to that.

Steve Jobs Was Kicked Out of the Company He Started

By the ripe age of thirty, Steve Jobs was incredibly successful, wealthy, and famous. He'd revolutionized the world and created an iconic brand. Even so, he was later forced out of the billion-dollar company that he had built into an empire. "I was out—and very publicly out," he recalled in his commencement speech at Stanford University. "What had been the focus of my entire adult life was gone, and it was devastating." He added, "I was a very public failure." But he did not let the defeat stop him, and he didn't take it too personally. Eventually, Jobs was asked to come back to Apple Inc. because they were failing without him. When he returned, he brought Apple to new heights of success, and gave the world more unbelievable technology.

Babe Ruth Held the Record for Strikeouts

Babe Ruth, one of the greatest baseball hitters who ever lived, may have had a home run record of 714 during his career, but he still had a total of 1,330 strikeouts. At one point he held the world record for strikeouts. His opinion about this fact was, "Every strike brings me closer to the next home run."

Stephen King Received Thirty Rejections on His First Book

Stephen King gave up on his first book, *Carrie*, after receiving thirty rejections. However, after listening to his wife, he resubmitted the manuscript and *Carrie* was made into two movies. Also, after having hundreds of books published, King is one of the best-selling authors of all time. Together, his books have sold around 350 million copies.

Chapter 4

Quit Waiting

"Are you ready?" Klaus asked finally.
"No," Sunny answered.
"Me neither," Violet said, "but if we wait until we're
*   ready we'll be waiting for the rest of our lives,*
*   Let's go."*

—LEMONY SNICKET, *THE ERSATZ ELEVATOR*

Quit waiting . . .

   . . . for the perfect day.
   . . . to figure everything out.
   . . . for your boss to give you a raise (especially if you don't
   ask for it).
   . . . to get what you want if you don't write it down and
   make it happen.
   . . . for the right teacher.
   . . . for the resources.

. . . to ask for what you want.

. . . to get more sleep.

. . . for the economy to get better.

. . . for them to say thank-you first.

. . . for them to apologize first.

. . . to talk to that person you've always found attractive.

. . . to tell that person you love them.

. . . for your dreams to come true.

. . . to make the money you want to make.

. . . for the experience.

. . . for someone or something to save you.

. . . for the solutions to potential failures that may or may
  not happen someday.

. . . for someone to help you.

. . . for someone to do it for you.

Don't wait—it will be too late.

There are no guarantees in life, except for one thing—you will be swept clean off the face of this planet one day. The only thing promised in life is death. It may sound firm and harsh, but it's the truth. The good news is that what we do until this day comes is totally up to us. Nothing and no one can tell you how to best spend your time, not even your lover. Nobody knows what's best for you, even if they act like they know. All we really know is that we're born and then we die. All the time between is for you to fill in the blanks, for you to decide.

If you accept that one day you're going to die, it's much easier to steer your life in the right direction. Knowing that life won't last forever gives it more meaning. You won't always be able to touch, hear, taste, smell, see, create, express, and learn. I don't know why that is—I wasn't in on the original master plan of this planet—but I do think it's a good idea to come to terms with our temporary nature.

What do you want to leave behind after you are gone? If you knew you only had a few years left, how would you live your life? What would you do? What would you want people to know?

Perhaps death has become taboo because we're encouraged to live common and mediocre lives. If we face the fact that death will probably come sooner than we expect, we might want to change how we live our lives. But change involves a lot of courage, and even struggle—struggle that we don't want in a comfortable world. So we go on with our days as if they'll last forever. *I have plenty of time*, we think innocently.

Time is fleeting, so it's important to take advantage of it in the ways we see most fit. Thinking that we have an unlimited amount of time is an illusion that coaxes us into believing that we can procrastinate. We actually have no idea if we even have time—time is simply an idea.

I am writing this paragraph right now because I could die in my sleep tonight. It's totally possible. And it's important to me that you hear this work, so I write it. If, on the other hand, I knew that I wanted to write this work, but I didn't for x, y, or z reason, then it would build resentment and regret inside of me. So I don't leave my words unsaid.

Is there anything left unsaid inside of you?

I don't think you should die until you're ready, until you've wrung out every last bit of living that you can. But I don't make the decisions about this, and neither do you. So I suggest wringing out every last bit of living with the time you have today.

Do you think it's possible to be alive without living? If you were asking me, I'd say yes to this question. I'm not talking about whether or not your heart is beating, but rather, if you've made it beat in different cadences because of the adventures you've sought.

Often people don't seek out adventure because they believe lies about themselves. You know what I am talking about. There are millions of examples: the woman who thinks she's too old, the kid who thinks he's too young, the girl who thinks she isn't pretty enough, the man who thinks he isn't ready, the woman who thinks her boob size determines the quality of her life, the student who thinks intelligence is determined by test scores and grade point averages, the person who finds a stranger attractive yet finds not the courage to strike up a conversation.

The truth is that we all have flaws. But happy people, the successful few, are those who recognize their flaws, and continue to live in spite of them. They are aware that they'll die before they could ever resolve all of their flaws. So why wait? Why wait for the perfect body, partner, job, and clothes? Start living now. What you think you need to have before you begin will find you once you start. You simply need to have the courage to start living the life you desire today.

Some of you may use the excuse, "But I'm too busy to . . ." Whenever I think I'm too busy to follow my dreams, I ask myself, "What fits your busy schedule better? Seeing your family, telling someone that you love them, starting small by working at your goals a little each day, or feeling half-dead twenty-four hours a day, never having tried to take even little baby steps toward your dreams?

"Leave with the World" Exercise

Ask yourself the following question and write down your answers:

If you were to pass away today, will what you have left
with the world been all it could be? Why or why not?

Dying Regrets

Life is short, so the words of those who are dying are of great interest
to me. I am especially interested in their regrets, because hearing
them gives us an opportunity. We can listen and decide which of
their regrets are important to our own lives—it's an opportunity to
learn from what others consider to have been their mistakes.

I hear Loren Nancarrow's final words again and again (he's the
father of my good friend, whom I discussed in the introduction to
this book). And when I think about Vic (my friend who died,
whom I also discussed in the introduction to this book), I immediately think about what he would have said if he knew he were
going to die.

I will never know what Vic would have said, but because
Loren's words were so encouraging I decided to read *The Top
Five Regrets of the Dying*, a book written by Bronnie Ware, a pallia-
tive nurse who recorded the most common regrets of the dying.
The top five regrets that she discovered were:

1. I wish I'd had the courage to live a life true to myself,
   not the life others expected of me.

   "This was the most common regret of all. When
   people realize that their life is almost over and look

back clearly on it, it is easy to see how many dreams have gone unfulfilled. Most people had not honored even a half of their dreams and had to die knowing that it was due to choices they had made, or not made."

2. I wish I hadn't worked so hard.

"There is nothing wrong with loving your work and wanting to apply yourself to it. But there is so much more to life. Balance is what is important, maintaining balance."

3. I wish I'd had the courage to express my feelings.

". . . to be in any sort of relationship where you do not express yourself, simply to keep the peace, is a relationship ruled by one person and will never be balanced or healthy."

4. I wish I had stayed in touch with my friends.

"Often they would not truly realize the full benefits of old friends until their dying weeks and it was not always possible to track them down. Many had become so caught up in their own lives that they had let golden friendships slip by over the years. There were many deep regrets about not giving friendships the time and effort that they deserved. Everyone misses their friends when they are dying."

5. I wish that I had let myself be happier.

"Life doesn't owe us anything. We only owe ourselves, to make the most of the life we are living, of
the time we have left, and to live in gratitude."

Which of these regrets speaks the most to you? Are there a
few? What changes can you make in your life today to ensure that
you don't feel this way when you die?

Make a Difference

The purpose of life is not to be happy. It is to be useful, to be
honorable, to be compassionate, to have it make some difference that you have lived and lived well.

—Ralph Waldo Emerson

Do you remember Martin Luther King Jr.'s famous speech "I've
Been to the Mountaintop"? Here are a few lines: "And He's allowed
me to go up to the mountain. And I've looked over and I've seen
the Promised Land. I may not get there with you. But I want you
to know tonight that we, as a people, will get to the Promised
Land. And so I'm happy tonight. I'm not worried about anything.
I'm not fearing any man."

He gave that speech on April 3, 1968, and died the next day,
on April 4, 1968. I think if we look at his words closely, there's no
way he didn't know he was going to be killed the next day. "I may
not get there with you . . . I'm not fearing any man." I believe he
knew what was happening. Now I know there's no way to prove

this, but I believe he knew that he was going to get killed, but he wasn't worried.

If your intention is to make a difference in the world (like Martin Luther King Jr.'s was), you can overcome any fear, and any challenge that you are facing. Without a doubt MLK Jr. was doing what he felt was the work of God—the work that produced the highest good for the world. Due to this fact, he felt an incredible power that was only available to him because of his intention to serve the world. I believe that allowed him to go out and give a speech when he may have known he was going to be killed. Do you know how many times his life was threatened? Probably more times than we can ever imagine. Yet he remained unaffected. He said, "I'm not worried about anything." He wasn't worried about anything because he knew he was doing the right thing—the thing he was meant to do.

When you choose to live your life in service to make other people's lives better, what was once a fear becomes a speck on the horizon. It's hard to attach to fear when we're connected to other people and to service. When our lives are threatened we know that as long as we're doing what we're meant to do, we'll be okay, even if it means we have to die.

This same principle can be applied to Gandhi's life. He accomplished incredible things because he was supported by the vibrational power of wanting to make a difference. His enthusiasm was like an uncontrollable flame that couldn't burn out. He changed the world because he was clear about what he wanted, which was to make a difference. He stuck to his principles, didn't compromise on his vision, and didn't let up until the day of his assassination. (His follow-through is what led to his being killed, but I am sure he died proud of what he had accomplished.)

There are thousands of examples that prove that it's never impossible to reach your goals, to make a difference, to change the world. You just need to be brave and believe. Nothing is impossible if you are focused on how you can help other people.

Bob Marley once said, "My life is for the people. And if it's not, then I don't want my life." This was a reply to a reporter who asked him why he went out and played a free benefit concert in Jamaica for 300,000 people (even though he was shot the night before). The reporter said, "You know you could have been shot and killed when you went out there!" And he laughed, "Ha! What is to be must be." He spoke with an incredible power where the fear of death became irrelevant. Fear holds human beings back more than anything else. And when the fear of death is gone, people bring out their superhero qualities, which allow them to literally accomplish anything.

When his career took off, Bob Marley used to drive to downtown Trenchtown, one of the biggest ghettos in the world, where he would sit on the curb and give handfuls of money to people. Lines would go around the corner of the block, because he would give enough money to people so they could start something on their own. His life was dedicated to making a difference, which is what allowed him to overcome extremely adverse circumstances and poverty.

If you focus on how you can help, how you can serve other people, and how you can make the world a better place, nothing will be impossible for you. If you help people get what they want from life, you can get anything you want out of life. At least, that's what Zig Ziglar said, and I agree with him. You can get anything you want out of life if your focus is on how you can help other people do the same. If your focus is on how you can make a positive impact on the world, all that you want will be yours. You become powerful. You become strong when you become kind. When you are focused on how to make a difference, you find the genius within.

A New Golden Rule—Give to Others

No one is useless in this world who lightens the burdens of
another.

—Charles Dickens

Destiny is the path that finds you when you focus on improving
your life and the world around you. Life is better when you make
other people feel better. Giving is the prescription to happiness.
Disease comes from the false belief that you don't have anything to
give. Everyone has something to give. Something as simple as a
smile or giving your time to listen to someone else makes a difference. You have so many unique talents—use your imagination to
think about the special skills that only *you* can offer to others.

We all want to feel significant and we all search for meaning.
If you give to others, you will know that what you do in life makes
a difference. You will look at the faces of those you help and you
will know that you have touched their hearts.

The Belief That You Can't Make a Living Giving

People often believe that if they give too much, then they won't have
enough for themselves, and that giving things away will not fill up
their bank account. But I would like you to consider that the opposite is true—giving to others actually brings more into your life
and is the nature of business. A successful business offers something
of value to others' lives, and in exchange for that value, people (customers) pay for it. If you develop something, either within yourself
or externally, that creates value for people, and if you share it with

the world, you will make a living. This is the nature of giving and the nature of business.

Give Care, Give Hope

> I slept and I dreamed that life is all joy. I woke and I saw that life is all service. I served and I saw that service is joy.
>
> —Khalil Gibran

The first time I met Tom Shadyac, the director of movies such as *Ace Ventura, Liar, Liar,* and *Bruce Almighty,* as well as the documentary *I Am,* was at his first radio show with a live audience. There were about fifty people there. I sat in the front row and waited until everyone left so that I could talk privately with him. While waiting, I watched as everyone lined up to shake hands and talk with Shadyac. I was only about three feet away, so I could see that each person who approached him left the interaction with a huge smile. Some people really wanted to talk to him and share their story—he stayed present with each person, regardless of the long line behind them, the whole time. He gave each individual his full attention and always held eye contact. He allowed everyone to feel close to him—he grabbed their hands, patted them on the back, hugged them, smiled, and laughed with them. His ability to stay present was astonishing. I believe that it is hard to remain as humble, human, and connected as he was during these interactions. Many famous people are put on a pedestal, which goes straight to their ego, and it makes it impossible for them to truly connect with others. However, in spite of this fact, Shadyac was able to give his full attention to everyone.

Giving our *full* attention to others, and to tasks in life, is extremely demanding. If you believe you have nothing to give, start by focusing on giving your attention to others. It lets people know you care and that they matter.

While I watched Shadyac, I turned to his business manager, Harold, who happened to be sitting next to me.

"Wow. He really makes everyone feel so great," I said.

"You've barely seen anything yet. Tom regularly goes to a restaurant and spends ten dollars, but gives the waiters a hundred-dollar tip. I've seen people cry countless times because of his generosity," Harold said with a straight face. "Tom is so generous with his time and money that it's at a point where we try and warn him and tell him that he can't be *that* generous." Harold looked at me again very seriously, without a smile, and said, "I mean, I gave my kidney to a stranger and I thought that was nice. But Tom, he changes someone's life every day."

Witnessing Shadyac's interactions that day and hearing about his generosity helped me realize how many times I've told myself that I am too busy to help others. It helped me realize that I have limits on my love and on what I am willing to give, while Shadyac just keeps giving. Sure, he may have more money than me, but so do a lot of people, and most of them don't give so much of it away that their friends and family start to worry.

The next day, I helped Shadyac set up 250 brand-new bicycles and helmets on the playground of Foster Elementary School in Compton, Los Angeles. Tom bought a bike and a helmet for every single fifth grader at the school. For most of the kids, it was the only present they would receive that holiday season. "We're not giving you bikes and presents. We're letting you know that we love you, and that you matter, and that we care about you," Shadyac said to them in a short speech.

I watched as the children and their parents cried while he spoke.

It was clear to me that they were touched because Shadyac wasn't simply buying them something, he was letting them know that he did this because he really cared. Most of the time, caring is the only thing we need to give to change someone's world.

The World's Poorest President

No one has ever become poor by giving.

—Anne Frank, *The Diary of Anne Frank*

World leaders today are usually hidden behind gold-encrusted gates of mansions large enough to house small towns, with seas of armed guards that protect them and preserve their lavish lifestyles. They are disconnected from the poor and working classes, and wear clothing that costs more than what the majority of people make in a year. However, there is one leader who is different—José Mujica, the president of Uruguay, billed as the "World's Poorest President." According to many, this humble farmer, who wears worn-out clothing and sandals, has more resemblance to a hobbit than he does to the majority of today's presidents. José is seventy-eight years old and gives 90 percent of his salary to charity. He lives an extremely casual life, and lives in what some consider a run-down farmhouse. He has only two police officers who watch his dirt road, where other farmers reside.

"They say I am the poor president. No, I am not a poor president. Poor people are those who always want more and more, those who never have enough of anything. Those are the poor. Because they are in a never-ending cycle and they won't ever have enough time in their lives. I choose this austere lifestyle. I choose not to have too many belongings so that I have time to live the way I want to live," Mujica says.

Mujica rejected a state palace to live in his farmhouse, and drives an old Volkswagen Beetle. And even though he loves his lifestyle, Mujica never encourages or forces anyone to live as he does. "If I asked people to live as I live, they would kill me," he said during an interview in his small, yet cozy, one-bedroom home.

Many of us want to be role models and leaders. But with a life of great importance comes great responsibility. You must lead by example, and live with congruence between your words and actions. If you wish to inspire others on a large scale, or even simply have the respect of your friends and family, you must be an example. You will live a meaningful life when you are an example of what is possible—what is possible when people stand up for what they believe in. Of what is possible when people realize their full potential. An example of what is possible when one lives their life to make other people's lives better.

If you believe in something with all your heart, do it. There's no need to convince and persuade others to follow you or to do it with you. Just do it for yourself because you know it's right. It doesn't matter what it is, as long as you know that you should live that way, do it.

Entrepreneurs: Social Visionaries

Entrepreneurs are very important people because they are the social visionaries of our society. However, they need to be extremely conscious of what they are trying to create. If an entrepreneur's mission statement is "fixing problems," they are relying on a broken world to make their living. We don't need entrepreneurs who want to fix a broken world. We need entrepreneurs whose mission is to create possibilities for others, especially in places where people did not think it was possible. This may seem like simply another form of offering solutions to people's problems, but it is important to be conscious of the way we think about what we do. Everything we do in life is propelled by energy, and our minds create vibrations based on our beliefs about the meaning of the words we use. That's why it is much more powerful and positive to make our mission about creating possibilities rather than fixing problems.

If we keep thinking *problem, problem, problem, problem . . . need to find solution*, we're going to end up simply creating more problems. If you are focused on the negative, even if it's to find solutions to it, you are going to create more negative. If, on the other hand, the mind is focused on a word like *possibilities*, a whole different level of emotional possibility opens up. The word *possibility* doesn't have the same type of constraints and negative implications that solving *problems* has.

If entrepreneurs and innovators focus on creating new possibilities for people, they do magnificent things for the world. When entrepreneurs do that, people say, "Wow, that person's light years ahead of their time." And if their focus is on their mission, they won't care if they're ahead of their time or not. They will focus on their mission, create possibilities for others, and will eventually be recognized for all the good that they do.

To be an entrepreneur, you must be an innovator, and to be an innovator, you must create and usher the new—rather than duplicate. The old paradigms and ways of doing things become obsolete only when new possibilities are available. Entrepreneurs have to convince people why they should try something different.

Stop thinking that there are problems that you need to solve— just present new possibilities. Thinking just in terms of problems can only lead to the destruction of the world, because it perpetuates the problems that already exist—advertising makes a fortune from selling thousands of subpar solutions to people's problems. A lot of the time the only difference between products is marketing or packaging. The results are the same—more money spent by the consumer without the problems being totally solved. And society can't continue to have the same problems that we have now, or our civilization will die off within the next 100 years. The goal in launching a product can't just be to get as many people to buy it under any semi-ethical practices—the goal can't just be to see what problems consumers have, then flush another subpar product out in different packaging to generate more revenue in a booming industry. New possibilities and ways of doing things need to be ushered, created, presented, and brought to life. And they need to be brought to life *by you*! An entrepreneur recognizes that we should not feed on problems, but present solutions to make life more livable. They focus on the possibilities that make life more enjoyable *while* we are living it.

An entrepreneur's responsibility is to create something so different—with so much value, life, possibilities, and intention—that other people just can't resist stepping into a new way of living. Something so great that the rest of us simply can't resist letting go of our problems, old habits, dated ways of seeing and doing things, and unnecessary ways of treating ourselves and others. When entrepreneurs convince people to do that, the world is given a piece of peace.

If you want to be an entrepreneur, you must feel the future that your product, company, dream, idea, or invention can create. You have to *feel* that future so strongly and fully that it's as though you've already created it—a real solution—then the money to back that intention will come

"Future Life" Exercise

First you have to "be" it. Then you go "do" it. And last you can "have" it. Making big dreams realities means being that big person first. You don't just get what you want, you get what you are. To create the future that you want to create, to make your dreams come true, you must stay connected to the feelings that you want to create before they are real in your current reality. Everything that happens in your life is created by the stories that you tell yourself—by who you are being and how you are thinking and what you're giving your attention to. So dream bigger dreams for yourself and for the world, even while you are living in your current reality, which may be very different from where you are trying to go. So be a bigger person than you've ever been. Become who you want to be before it even happens. When you become "it," then everything you want and need is there.

Imagine who you must be to live the life of your dreams—and then use your focus to be that type of person even before you reach those dreams of yours. Using your imagination is not a mystical, "la-la" extracurricular activity—it is like oiling the engine that makes everything go. Even Albert Einstein once said, "Logic will get you from A to B, but imagination will take you everywhere." And that imagination is always running—so the question is, where do you want to go and who do you want to be?

Your imagination works consciously, subconsciously, super-consciously, and probably even on many other levels that we do not yet have names for. The machine is always on—listening to what we have to say to ourselves! And often when we start exploring these ideas, our mind tells us that our imagination can't do all of these things, that it doesn't create reality. But guess what—you are imagining that! You've literally just chosen to imagine that. Do you see? Do you see that it's all up to you—that you can decide what to believe? Thoughts come from our imagination and you can decide which ones to choose.

So how do you get started in living the life of your dreams? How do you become the social visionary or entrepreneur of your own life? You do this by going into a vision state. You must imagine what type of person you will become in living your most heartfelt dreams—how you will act, what you will think, how you will treat yourself and others. Imagine what life could be like for you. Imagine who you can become. Not how it is now, but how it could be.

Give yourself ten to fifteen minutes to really feel what it will be like to be who you can be and go where you can go. Get up and act it out if you need to. Focus on the sensory experience, and when you feel like it has really dropped into your body, mind, heart, and spirit you can come back to reality. And coming back to reality is actually the trickiest part of this exercise. You *must* stay connected to who you want to be and what you want to create. You must try to stay connected despite all the problems you may have with the people, places, and patterns that make up your current life experience. This is a difficult challenge, but one that all innovators attempt to accomplish.

Chapter 5

Write It Down; Make It Happen

In an audio program created by one of my favorite authors, Jack Canfield, he says, "Make a list of the top one hundred and one things you want to do in life. And just believe that they will happen." The night I heard that, I made my list, and number nine was to become friends with and learn from Jack Canfield. I wanted to meet him because he is the creator of the Chicken Soup for the Soul series, which has sold about 500 million copies. However, I had some major obstacles in reaching this goal—I didn't know him or how to get in touch with him. Canfield isn't the type of guy who has his e-mail address on his website with an invitation to personally contact him. Nevertheless, I had made my list, trusted his words, and believed that someday it would happen. Then, six months later, in March 2013 (just before my first book, *Into the Wind*, was set to release), I got word that Canfield would be speaking at a charity event, so I bought the ticket online that week.

The day of the event I drove from my home in San Diego up to Los Angeles to the Beverly Wilshire Hotel. I was underdressed in a room full of very successful middle-aged people. I'd decided to be overly ambitious, and had signed a copy of my book to Canfield, with the belief that we'd meet that night. However, when the event started, I realized that there were three or four hundred people there, and *everyone* wanted to meet Canfield. There were lines to take pictures with him, but I didn't want to simply take a picture with him—I wanted enough time to talk with him and tell him how much he'd inspired me.

Canfield spent most of the night onstage. I began to panic, wondering if I'd ever get the one-on-one time that I desired. Then, he finished up a section of his talk to head back to his seat. I watched as he stepped off the stage—people shook his hand, asked for pictures, and wouldn't leave him alone. Then, I saw him go to his assigned table in the center of the ballroom floor. I watched from the higher level of seating, six or seven stairs above. In that moment I realized that it might be my only chance. I walked down the stairs, toward his seat. I looked at him sitting with five or six other people, and I decided to approach him. I tapped him on his left shoulder, "Excuse me, Jack, my name is Jake. I am twenty-one years old and I wrote this book." I handed him the book. "You inspired it." He smiled and held the book. "Oh, yeah? How did I inspire you?"

"A lot of ways," I replied. "But what comes to mind first is that although so many companies declined to publish your first book, you still succeeded. In your books you say, 'When someone says *no*, you must say *next*.' You said, 'Sw. Sw. Sw. Sw. Some will. Some won't. So what? Someone is waiting.' So when everyone told me *no*, I just kept going because I knew someone was waiting to help me."

Jack smiled big, and I knew he appreciated what I had said. He looked through the book. "This is a cool book," he said. "You've got to meet my wife. . . ." He turned to the woman to his right. It was his wife, Inga. We all began talking for a while. I stood next to Jack while they sat. Then, I found out Jack's wife and my mom went to high school together in La Jolla, San Diego. We talked for about ten minutes.

The next thing I knew the waiter was behind me. "Excuse me, sir," he said as he reached past me to put the preordered dinners on the table. *Dang! They are serving dinner now . . . looks like that's all the time I have with him*, I thought to myself. I started to wrap up the conversation because I didn't want to be rude, as their dinners were now in front of them. Then Jack looked at me standing next to him. "Are you going to eat that?" he asked. I looked at him with a puzzled expression on my face. He pointed to a plate by the seat in front of me. "No one is sitting there now. You should eat dinner with us." I smiled and tried my best to contain my excitement and act calm. Eight months earlier I had written that I wanted this to happen on a piece of paper, and now it was happening. . . .

A couple months later Jack gave me an endorsement for *Into the Wind*, which read, "*Into the Wind* is one wonderful Chicken Soup for the Soul story. . . ." And four months later, I found myself invited to stay the night at Jack's for his birthday party. There were about ten of us, including Jack and his wife. When dinner was served, I sat as close to Jack as I could. Finally, I got the nerve to ask him questions. "What's the one thing that's most important for young people to know? What's that one piece of advice you want them to know?" I asked him. He looked at me for a second . . . and then said, "Write it down. Make it happen." I looked at him feeling like his answer was incomplete; it was too short and simple. I nodded to let him know that I wanted him to keep talking. "That's it. Write down what you desire clearly. Then make it happen. You have everything you need to realize your dreams within you. If not, you wouldn't have had the desire in the first place."

I remember waking up in the morning and wishing that he had told me more. But, when I think about it now, what else is there to know? It's so clear; the people who impact the world the most, who become the most successful and the most fulfilled, are those who clearly know what they want. They are those who set goals that coincide with their overarching vision. They write them down and trust that they wouldn't have had the desire for those dreams if they couldn't turn them into a reality.

Just look at Jack. Throughout his life he has sold hundreds of millions of books and has impacted the lives of all the people who have bought them. He is honestly really happy, and none of what has happened to him is by chance or luck—it's exactly what he wanted. His life is what he intended it to be—it's what he wrote down. He accomplished the exact goals that he set for himself because after he wrote them down, he made them happen.

While I write this book (which, you now know, Jack wrote the Foreword to), I now understand the true meaning behind what he said on his birthday. He wanted me to know that success is simple, and making a difference is simple. It may not always be easy, but it is simple. Be clear. Write it down. Make it happen.

Writing Down Your Goals

Do you write down your goals? Do you know exactly what your goals are, right now? If you answered "no" to these questions, you are not alone. Not many of us have written them down. We've never tried, so we aren't aware that writing down our goals reinforces our commitment to them—it helps us focus, and it keeps us accountable for their fruition.

When I lived with my mom, she would often go to the store to buy groceries. I always knew when she had forgotten her grocery list because she would be back at the house really quickly. Having goals and not writing them down is like shopping without a list. Except in the case of goals it's even worse—we're living without moving toward what we enjoy most.

If you are hesitant to believe the importance of *writing down your goals*, go and ask a few of the happiest and also most successful people you know if they write down theirs. I have never met a happy and successful person who doesn't.

Here are some tips for writing down your goals. They need to be:

- Clear and specific—So a stranger would know what you meant.
- Attainable—Some may find them totally unrealistic, but if you believe they can come true, then write them down anyway.
- Dated—Some people believe goals should always be bound to time. I believe that some do and some don't (you'll know best which do and which don't).
- Tractable—You need to see if you're progressing or regressing.

Also, while setting your goals, remember that they're pointless unless you can take actionable steps toward them every day. They should be big enough that they make you feel a bit worried, but within the reach of incredible dedication.

Remember, the most important part is not what you can tangibly receive from achieving this goal or outcome—the most important part is the intangible personal growth that you will receive, and which will sustain your spirit. Do not be afraid to set a goal and to, as Henry David Thoreau once said, "Move confidently in the direction of your dreams."

Why Have Goals?

> If you're bored with life—you don't get up every morning with a burning desire to do things—you don't have enough goals.
>
> —Lou Holtz

We plan our vacations more consciously than we plan our lives— perhaps this is because it's easier to escape than it is to challenge ourselves. However, by doing this we are missing the whole point of life. In the long run, it's actually much easier to build a life you love than to live a life you feel you must escape from. People take vacations or get drunk on the weekends to stay sane enough to re- turn to the life they hate, and sadly many of them live this way their entire lives, which is sure to lead to regrets when they die.

I don't know why so many of us live life without thinking about our goals and desires. I don't know why we don't set clear goals, write them down, and put them into action like we do with vacation planning. But I don't think the "why" matters. What matters is that we need to be setting more potent goals—goals that inspire and challenge us. We need to set goals that we don't think we can achieve.

Do you find that you are bored with life—that you don't wel- come each day with a fierce desire to stretch yourself? Do you find that you don't have goals, or perhaps that you don't set big enough goals for yourself? If you answered "yes" to any of these questions, then let me ask you one more: *Don't you want more passion, motivation, inspiration, and meaning in your life?* Like holding a magnifying glass to the sun and watching its rays channel precisely onto what you want with increased power, goals direct the energy of life toward where you want it to go. *Goals concentrate our energy to maximize our passions, power, and purpose.*

Many of us hardly live because we forget that we are the energetic, creative force that directs our lives. Sure, good things do come to those who wait, but great things come to those who work their butts off, to those who are looking to *improve* and *grow*. No matter what stage of life you are in there are always opportunities to learn, grow, and improve. "Grow and improve what?" you may ask. Well, it's the one thing that can always improve and grow— your *character.*

The more we challenge ourselves and uncover who we are, the more we discover what we're made of and capable of, which creates more excitement for life! Even pain, heartbreak, and frustration have their innate importance in growth and improvement by what we can learn from them!

This is why it doesn't matter if you're a person with little talent and education or a brilliant genius with a Harvard degree, the person with the clearest, most focused direction and goal will go the furthest. All of us arrive somewhere, so before you get anywhere, decide where you want to go.

Where do you want to go? I know that is a question we're not used to being asked. But we can no longer use social conditioning as an excuse to justify mediocrity. I, at least, choose to do that no longer. And I hope that you do make this choice with me.

What do you want? You have to know before you take steps toward getting it. And remember, you don't need to want a thing. Needing material things is simply another holdup that our system has put into our minds. Forget things, and think about feelings.

What do you want to *feel*? This is always a good place to start. A lot of times kids will come up to me after my speeches and say, "I don't know what I want. I don't know where to begin." And I always tell them that it doesn't really matter what they want. If you have the courage to keep trying new things, you'll eventually find the thing you are looking for. Besides, I think that what we all really want is adventure.

What are the things that make you feel adventurous? That make you feel alive? What are the activities that make you feel connected to yourself and others, to life, to your environment, and to the earth? Think about the moments in life that have made you stop and say, "Oh, wow, that was awesome!" Or, "Oh, wow, I'm alive!"

If the things that have made you feel this way have been extremely debilitating or addictive, I invite you to channel the energy you put into them into courage—courage that helps you make the next decision about where you want to go in life. Energy that helps you become who you think you want to be and to try things that you think could make you feel alive.

Ultimately we all just want to feel good—it's that plain and simple. It's the reason we want money, take drugs, and have sex. Feeling good is the reason why we do anything that we do in life.

Would you believe me if I told you that the secret to feeling good is simply to be who you want to be? Don't think that it can be that simple? Try it. Ask yourself, "Who do I want to be?" When we get clear about the type of person we want to be, we start living from that place, from the integrity of the vision that we have about ourselves. And when we live with integrity, we build confidence. We begin to attract the type of friendships that fulfill our heart and soul, which propels the momentum of our dreams. And then, when our minds measure our progress, we define what is happening as success, which is a big part of feeling happy.

But don't confuse this type of success with the type that our American culture asks us to seek (that is, having the most things or winning a prize in the competition). The type of success that I'm referring to measures progress (how far one comes and where they're going) against one's own abilities. It's the art of taking the time to recognize that we've come a long way, even when it's simply from A to B. And then being proud when we get to C, and being okay when we fall back to B, because eventually we get to L, and oh great, now we've made it to Y. Oops, back to P . . . which all eventually brings us to Z, our goal. And when we reach the goal, we also have to be willing to start over again, moving from A to B to C to D to C to L to N to P . . . this is a cycle that continues as long as we want to progress and grow in our lives.

This process is the only one that will leave you feeling deeply fulfilled in life. Some of you won't want to hear that. Hearing this may even make you want to close this book. But, for those of you who can accept this, ask yourselves, "Where is it that I want to go from here? Do I want to take the *same* pill, or do I want to take the *new* pill?" And by "pill," I simply mean your view of yourself and the world—your perception of what's possible, your beliefs that it's okay for you to have dreams and pursue them. It's the mind-set you can live in that knows no limits.

If you take the same pill, you will do the same thing that you have been doing over and over again. It's brought you to where you are now, so it hasn't failed you. But it will keep giving you what you already have, which might be nice, but you are entitled to more.

You can have more from yourself and more from life! More success! More fun! More happiness! You can have more wonderful experiences, and feel more excitement in your relationships with people, places, and things. But you can't have any of this until you are connected with yourself. Which is what the new pill, the limitless mind-set can give you—a new way to look at yourself as a powerful person who can overcome challenges and is more than capable to make your dreams happen! The only requirement for taking the new pill, to be a no-limit type of person, however, is personal responsibility and honesty about what you really want. You will have the responsibility of taking the actions needed to be who you want and live how you want. Those actions can be anything from writing a book to meeting new friends, from feeding a homeless person on the street to writing down some goals.

If you don't know where to begin, start by thinking about how you can help someone else. If you get out there and help just one person, you'll see that the actual value in life comes from being of service to others. When we realize this, life naturally finds more meaning. We feel responsible for making the world a better place.

For a lot of us, that's heavy! Our society hasn't set us up for responsibility. We aren't taught how to really take care of ourselves. We're a world at war and have destroyed a lot of the planet and of one another. But we can't blame a culturally irresponsible world for the lack of responsibility that we take in our own lives. We need to tell ourselves a new story. From this point forward, we must choose to uncover things that are going to make us and others feel good. We must be the type of people we wish to be, not hope that it happens someday. We must eat healthful, good food; take care of the planet and one another; take only what we need; and make what we know in our hearts to be the right choices. This is why choosing who you want to be, and living with integrity, is so important.

We avoid these choices our entire lives. We hypnotize ourselves for hours a day with sitcoms, reality TV shows, and Facebook; we take drugs; eat processed food, sugar, and candy; we buy things we don't need (or want); we have sex with people we don't really respect; we go places we don't like to be seen with people we want to be around with even less. Yes, there are distractions galore. This list could go on and on, and I'm sure you can think of many other things to add to it. The important thing is to be aware of what you are doing, and to ask yourself if this is really what you want from yourself.

I know it can be hard to know what you want. We have created a world that encourages you to want what everyone else wants—where many of us believe that "life is a bitch, then you die." But again, only you can be responsible for your life.

So, where do you want to go? Know the answer. It's the fuel that will get you there, because it's fuel made by *you*.

"Thirty Things" Exercise

In Jack Canfield's book *The Success Principles,* he asks you to write down:

- Thirty things you want to be
- Thirty things you want to have
- Thirty things you want to do

I encourage you to do this exercise. It will probably not be easy—you may get stuck while writing, but challenge yourself to keep going. Remember to make your goals clear—a stranger should be able to read them and know what you mean.

When you finish, go back through what you wrote and put an asterisk next to a few items on each page—next to the ones that are *really* calling you. Then, make those your primary focus for how-ever long it takes for you to make them happen. Also, a good way to keep your goals on the top of your mind is to tape the paper you wrote them down on onto your wall. Read it and refresh your mind on what you wrote at least once a week.

The goals with the asterisks are your conscious goals. Leave the rest of the goals for your subconscious to manifest for you. But don't wait too long. When you achieve a conscious goal, cross it off the list, and then find a subconscious goal, and bring it to the fore-front. Help make each goal happen with conscious and consistent action. Keep this process moving forward until you have reached all of your goals. And continue to add new goals whenever you please, whenever a new desire burns inside of you.

"Ideal Life" Exercise

Get out a few sheets of paper (or a journal if you have one available) and answer this question: If I was living my ideal life—my dream life—what would be happening in my life one year from now? Allow yourself to freewrite, and don't stop until you have written everything down.

This exercise is the first step in turning your imagination into reality. Why let your life create your dreams when your dreams can create your life? If you allow your dreams to create your life, then your life will have more meaning. You will help create what happens to you rather than just watching what happens to you. It's time to stop wishing you could lose weight, make more money, or live a more fulfilling life—just do it now. Participate in the cre-ation of your life.

Subconscious Programming

The person with a fixed goal, a clear picture of his desire, or an ideal always before him, causes it, through repetition, to be buried deeply in his subconscious mind and is thus enabled, thanks to its generative and sustaining power, to realize his goal in a minimum of time and with a minimum of physical effort. Just pursue the thought unceasingly. Step by step you will achieve realization, for all your faculties and powers become directed to that end.

—Claude M. Bristol

Writing down what you want allows you to program your subconscious mind. Psychologists tell us that 95 percent of our lives are governed by our subconscious mind. That means that the unconscious part of us is running the show, or in other words, our life is on autopilot. *Our life is created from the information we have stored in our memory.*

This is why writing down our dreams and goals is so important. When you write something down, it gets stored in your subconscious mind and goes directly into your memory. You are seeing it with your eyes while you write it, and your muscles are shaping the letters and writing the words. Your mind is getting excited thinking about it, and the emotion of what you write gets imprinted into your imagination.

Studies show that we remember about 80 percent of the information that we write down, and that we only remember about 8 percent of the information that we don't write down. So it seems reasonable to conclude that the same must be true for our desires. If we don't write them down, we forget them, there isn't enough focus on them, and the subconscious can't help create them. They aren't clear and strong enough to become reality. On the other hand, due to the fact that you are more likely to remember information you have written down, if you can take the initiative to write your dreams on paper, then your mind is aware of what you want and can help make it a reality.

The story about my relationship with Jack Canfield is a perfect example. Think about how many other things had to be lined up and working properly on a subconscious level for that to happen. I wrote it down months before. My subconscious mind immediately began working to turn it into reality. Then, when the night actually came, I had the impulse to go introduce myself many times before I actually did. That was because the impulse was not strong enough to catapult me into action. And when the feeling was finally strong enough to take action, I got up, but I had no idea that the waiters were behind the scenes getting the food ready for Canfield's table out of the hundreds of other tables they could have been waiting on. I had no idea that ten minutes after I started talking to Canfield the waiters would serve him while I was standing there. And I certainly didn't know that although there was not a single empty seat in the whole ballroom, the person who should have been sitting at Jack's left happened to go home early and didn't eat dinner, so there was an empty seat right next to him.

In fact, I didn't even notice that empty seat until the waiter put the food down and served everyone. And the waiter had no idea that no one was sitting there anymore, or he wouldn't have put the food down in the first place. Canfield was the only one who noticed and that's why he asked me to eat with him.

Who could have thought up that scenario so perfectly? Not me . . . it truly was perfect. I could have walked over there ten minutes earlier and I might have never had the opportunity to speak with him. And what if I arrived at his table ten minutes later? I probably would've missed the waiter and wouldn't have had the opportunity to eat with Canfield. I didn't figure out how to make that all work—my subconscious mind did. But it was only able to help me because I consciously wrote out what I wanted, and I believed that it was possible. Writing it down and believing were what allowed this amazing experience to occur.

There's nothing special about me and there's nothing special about this process. All I know is that it works. Your job is to write down what you want, and when opportunities present themselves, take action.

"Subconscious Programming" Exercise

Here are some ways that Jack Canfield and I recommend programming your subconscious:

1. Change your passwords (e-mail, phone, home, social media, and wherever else you have them) to words that spark positivity every time you type them. Use words that give you confidence.

2. Inspect your room and look at everything in it, including posters, paintings, sheets, wallpaper, rugs, books, and pictures. Get rid of anything and everything that evokes negative energy. Then, replace them with items that are more positive. Buy candles, posters, and pictures that make you feel good. Surround yourself with colors that you like. And if you don't have any money to buy new things, don't worry. You can draw positive images, create decorations

yourself, or simply move things you already have around. Restock your room so that it empowers you. It should be a power haven where you recharge yourself and align with your vision. Surround yourself with inspiration and help yourself feel connected to your dreams.

3. Now take a walk around your house and do the same thing. Is there a sofa that bothers you? A table you don't want there? Is the carpet dirty? Do the pictures on the refrigerator or wall bring up less than optimal feelings? Get rid of or rearrange whatever you don't like. (And buy some fresh flowers!)

4. Go through your closet and do the same thing you did with your house, but this time with your clothes. Does your clothing suit your energy? Only keep the items that you truly love.

5. Check the screen saver and desktop on your computer and phone—make sure they have positively enhancing images.

6. Don't listen to music with lyrics that don't create positive images. Listen to music that makes you feel good.

7. Don't read books, articles, magazines, and newspapers that are not inspiring, educational, and encouraging. Find news that lifts you up, rather than brings you down.

8. Choose a sound for your cell phone ringtone and alarm clock that you like. You want to receive calls and start your day with a positive vibe.

9. Get a poster/whiteboard and make a vision board. This is a place where you post photos, magazine cutouts, and write positive ideas about your life, yourself, or

your dreams. Put the vision board in a place that is visible upon opening your eyes in the morning. Even if you wake up feeling anxious or stressed, these positive images will go into your subconscious mind and work their magic.

10. Put inspirational quotes on your bathroom mirror so that when you brush your teeth or wash your face, you are inspired.

Chapter 6

Personal Responsibility

*If you could kick the person in the pants responsible
for most of your trouble, you wouldn't sit for a month.*

—THEODORE ROOSEVELT

"My dad stabbed me." My close friend went on to explain his relationship with his father: "He used to beat me up when I was asleep, and then in the morning he would say, 'I was just drunk.' And both of my parents would tell me I was stupid even though I had straight A's."

I was shocked when one of my best friends finally revealed these intimate details of his upbringing. Both of his parents were severe alcoholics who beat him nearly every day. They abused him both physically and emotionally. His parents would even hit him when he got a B on a test. So when he was seventeen years old, he decided to move out of his parents' house. He preferred homelessness to living with them. He explained that he could've become an alcoholic like his parents, blaming them for his disease, or he could've wasted his life and blamed it on his past, but he chose not to. He knew that how his life would end up was his choice. He knew that no matter how much pain he felt, he didn't have to keep feeling it. In his heart and mind he forgave his parents, although he knew that he didn't need to tell them that or see them anymore.

While homeless, he started his own business. He is now only twenty-one years old with a six-figure income. He is one of the kindest and most understanding people I've ever met. He explains how he became this person: "I could've chosen to make no money and blame my parents, or whatever else, but instead, I slept four hours a night on the floor, working eighteen-hour days for a year. And now I am living the life I love and I am at peace with my past and with my parents. They are not responsible for how I live my life. I can choose to move on if I want to."

My friend asked me not to use his name when sharing this story. He doesn't want his past to create his future. He took matters into his own hands and changed his life, shaping it to his liking.

Even so, his story is the perfect example of what J. K. Rowling explained during her 2008 commencement speech at Harvard University: "There is an expiry date on blaming your parents for steering you in the wrong direction; the moment you are old enough to take the wheel, responsibility lies with you." This is often difficult to accept. If you can't blame your parents, then whom can you blame—your friends, your genes? No. No one. You can't blame anything. You've made your own choices. You've allowed yourself to be where you are—to work as much (or as little) as you do, to take (or not to take) care of your health and the shape of your body, to be intelligent (or unintelligent), to feel good (or not good) about yourself, and to make the income you receive. You are responsible for the results in all areas of your life.

Some of you may be saying, "But what about what happened?"

Or, "What about what *they* did?" Someone may have done something, or something may have happened to you, but it is *your* responsibility to keep going, to make different choices, and to change your life if you don't like it. You are 100 percent responsible.

Many of us like to take responsibility only when things are going well. However, this is actually a powerless belief system. It is more empowering to have responsibility all of the time, even when things aren't going well, because then we can change them and have control over how our lives progress.

Why Taking Responsibility Is Important

> The victim mind-set dilutes the human potential. By not accepting personal responsibility for our circumstances, we greatly reduce our power to change them.
>
> —Steve Marabol

Responsibility is a prerequisite for a purpose-driven life. Who is responsible for your ability to live the life you've imagined? It's not the responsibility of parents, schools, friends, strangers, or life itself to make life work for you. You are the only being on this planet who knows what you see within the gates of your imagination. You are the only one who knows what you really want to do with your life, and you are the only one who can make your dreams come true.

It's no one's fault but your own if you've failed to go in the direction of your dreams. And yes, this remains true regardless of the fact that someone told you that your dream was impossible, or rejected you the first few times you tried to make it come true—you are the one who chooses to believe in those words over the power of your own dreams. You are the one who chose to do what you have done with your life. If you chose to blame the shortcomings of your life on your family or the past, and tell everyone that you felt pressured to do what you are doing, or you feel that life is out to get you, then, well, it's your loss. The truth is that it's your responsibility to be strong enough to say *no* to things you don't want to do. It's your responsibility to tell yourself a new story about what is possible for your life. It's your responsibility to focus on the positive, be grateful, and love yourself. This is a much more productive use of your psychology than worrying about why everything is doomed and why you can't do something.

Eventually, we must all accept that it's our own thoughts, beliefs, reactions, actions, and inactions that determine our individual lives. It's not Mom and Dad's fault—even if they were "the worst parents ever." And we cannot blame our circumstances—the cards we were dealt—for the result of our lives either. Remember my friend's story? There are countless other examples of people who have achieved their dreams with similar or worse-off starting points and scenarios.

Take responsibility and stay positive. Keep going, forgive, and improve. Jim Rohn—American entrepreneur, author, and motivational speaker—once said, "Don't wish life was easier, wish you were better." And become better! After all, there are only two choices in life: accept things as they are and subject yourself to a life you hate, or accept responsibility, change things, and live a life you love.

The Consequences of Lack of Responsibility

The final forming of a person's character lies in their own hands.

—Anne Frank

Not taking responsibility for your actions leads to stress and depression. Life is much better when you admit your mistakes and weaknesses—doing so is an act of self-love. Most of us are guilty of waking up knowing that there are things to do, yet cringing at the sheer thought of such responsibility. To avoid these daily tasks, we pull our heads back under the covers and go back to sleep. Also, the majority of us have surfed the Web to postpone doing what we actually need to be doing. And almost all of us have turned the television on when we know that it isn't the best use of our time.

When we make choices such as these we forget that the meaning and purpose that we search for in life comes from consistent progress. Some days, that means we need to get out of bed, even when we are tired, to get all the little things done. Doing so propels us forward toward more happiness, confidence, success, and peace. We must muster up deep courage and discipline instead of lounging out, surfing the Internet, reading another book (including this one), or oversleeping.

However, don't get me wrong—sleep and rest are also important for getting the little things done. Sometimes it is necessary to do nothing at all. But we all know the difference between procrastinating or avoiding, and relaxing and rejuvenating. Life has peaks and valleys and you know when you are at a peak that may require more action, sweat, time, and focus.

A purpose-driven life is not a destination you arrive at—it's an ongoing journey on the railroad of life. Sometimes your caboose gets off the track because you rush to do things too quickly, or, on the contrary, because you don't put in the hustle to get things done. When we don't live in tune with our own pace—what we really want to be doing—we form regrets and resentments, which eventually cause train wrecks. To keep the train moving steadily on the tracks, you must constantly check in with your gut. Ask yourself,

"Am I doing what I want/need to do to live the best possible life? How badly do I want to make a difference? How committed am I to living life on the terms that will make me feel most alive?" This will help you gauge whether or not it is time to stop, start, or finish what you are doing. Listening to this inner wisdom will help you improve the quality of your life and better your community.

Whenever I postpone something that I know needs to be done, regardless of whether or not I believe the action is mundane or exciting, it always builds stress and anxiety. Sometimes the feeling is immediate and sometimes it's delayed, but what remains constant is that I feel frustrated when I don't do what I feel called to do. It feels bad to ignore my gut feelings and not do what I know I ought to.

Ignoring our gut adds weight to our shoulders that doesn't need to be there. The longer you wait to do something you want or need to do, the more you disrespect yourself. While writing this book, I knew that I had to get it done and send it to the publisher. Personally, I enjoy writing and creating much more than I like editing—but when I did not put the same focus into organizing this book as I did into imagining and creating, I always felt frustrated with myself.

We can avoid discontentment and self-conflict by doing what is most important to our principles. If we don't, we are telling ourselves that our dreams are not important. We are also unconsciously telling ourselves that we aren't looking for more *meaning* in life. This message comes across because we *know* there's something important to do, that would make life much better for ourselves or someone else, but we ignore it. This is one of the worst forms of self-sabotage. And it can be applied to all areas of life: health, food choices, business and personal relationships, family matters, self-esteem, and personal growth. Whether it's not attending a meeting because you think it will be boring or not asking someone out because of fear of rejection, you are not only setting yourself up for failure, you are stifling your growth.

Being responsible means following the directions and signals that your gut sends you. Be discerning about which signals are the strongest and heed them even if your thoughts tell you not to. Listen to your feelings . . . and follow them.

Self-Sabotaging

[N]o one can ever save someone else, you know? We can only save ourselves. You know that, don't you?

—Carrie Jones, *Need*

One of my best friends used to call me "Flake" instead of "Jake." When I say I am going to do something and don't, he calls me "Flake." If I say I will clean my car, which I've told him and his wife before, and don't do it, he calls me "Flake." I appreciate it because he is calling me out in a light manner. I respect who he is and take what he has to say into consideration.

We all have many sides of ourselves. Some are not so ideal, like the "Flake" side of me, which is disorganized. I've actually read books on how to be more responsible. However, I am not sure if there is an exact formula for being more organized. My car is often extremely dirty, and even when I make a list and put cleaning my car on that list, there are just some things I don't get done even when I know I need to do them. I always get frustrated with myself, and sometimes I even talk down to myself. I get down on myself when I do not treat myself well. It causes me, and those around me, stress. That's why it's important to take personal responsibility for all aspects of your life, even when it feels like the tasks are mundane. When I don't do what I need to do and, in turn, get down on myself, I try to remember what I do well and focus on my positives. I am definitely hardheaded, and I don't always learn—I am still young and oftentimes immature.

When I launched my first book, *Into the Wind*, I made a series of videos. I wrote scripts for the videos and paid for them to be filmed and produced nicely. I put a lot of time and money into one video in particular. I was very proud of it and had my publicist promote it to get featured on other blogs. I was really thankful and happy because all the big blogs that share similar content were accepting and featuring the video. Then, the biggest blog site of this genre didn't take it—they said that it "wasn't their type."

My publicist forwarded me the president of the blog's rejection e-mail, and told me that this person was jealous of me. She felt that the video was great and that it was made with the same inspirational intention and style as the other content featured on the blog. I then became extremely upset. I told the president of the blog that if the video were made by another person in the industry, he would have accepted it, and I named two other people who I knew were friends with this person to prove my point. While doing this I had forgotten what motivational speaker Les Brown once said: "Don't burn your bridges, there's always another day, don't talk about their mama . . ." I didn't think about that at the time, and my publicist became furious with me. That was the first time I realized that it isn't a good idea to freak out at someone in business. I was really upset with myself at the time, but I realize that we all learn and grow and have to laugh at ourselves sometimes.

So, as you can see, little things can get me down and I get frustrated with myself. However, I still remain proud of the things I do well, like writing books and reaching big goals. And I use that energy to keep going when I make mistakes.

Ask yourself the following question: "How much does it mean to you to reach your goal?" If the answer is "a lot," or "everything," then you need to just get it done—there are no valid excuses.

If you are unsure about how important something is for you, then you need to picture your future without it. If you don't like the way the future would look, then change the future by taking responsibility *now*. But if the answer to the question "How much does it mean to reach your goal?" is "Not much," then I invite you to get a new goal, dream, or focus for your life that means "a whole lot." Try to work toward that which gives you meaning. We decide how important happiness and sense of purpose is to us, but it doesn't mean that you or I won't self-sabotage ourselves along the way.

"Responsibility" Exercise

1. Take a few minutes to visualize what your life would look like down the road if you don't take greater responsibility for things you know you should. How does your life look? How does it feel? How do you feel about yourself, knowing that you could've done more to create a better life, but didn't?
2. Decide if you want that life, or something more.
3. If you want something different from your life, then do what you need to do to get it done today; don't postpone things anymore. If you want the same, where can you at least get better as a person? Remember how life can be if you are proactive, and take full responsibility. Don't accept less than what you truly want and who you are.

"Gratitude" Exercise

Cultivate the habit of being grateful for every good thing that comes to you, and to give thanks continuously. And because all things have contributed to your advancement, you should include all things in your gratitude.

—Ralph Waldo Emerson

When we fail, we often begin to focus on all the things we don't have and forget about all the things we do have. And this is not a good tactic. It's near impossible to try again after failing if we feel that we have absolutely nothing to be thankful for. J. K. Rowling did just the opposite, and came back stronger after hitting rock bottom. She lifted herself up by focusing on what she still had—a dream, a daughter, and a typewriter. This gave her the strength to overcome failure.

So the next time you feel like you are a failure and can't accomplish what you would like to, make a list of ten to fifteen things in life you are grateful for. Then, read it out loud. And notice how different you feel.

Stop Blaming

Taking personal accountability is a beautiful thing because it gives us complete control of our destinies.

—Heather Schuck, *The Working Mom Manifesto*

Stop blaming. Give it up. Take 100 percent of the responsibility for your actions, not 74 percent, or even 99 percent. Don't take

responsibility only when life is good, or only when it's bad—you are responsible for your life at all times.

Jack Canfield says, "Act as if every bad thing that happened to you, you either created it, allowed it, or promoted it. This is powerful because if you created it, you can re-create life the way you want. If you've allowed it, you can stop it. And if you've promoted it, you can promote something else."

Start looking for solutions to problems, instead of simply talking about how big they are. "It's not an obstacle; it's a problem to be solved," says Mattie Christianson, a kid who Jack Canfield interviewed in one of his books who has no arms and no legs, yet who still played on a baseball team that ranked number two in its league. This is the attitude we need to move forward in life.

In Jack Canfield's *The Success Principles*, he talks about how we can control only three things:

1. Behavior—"The way we act and react to any situation or thought. All of our habits and choices of action."
2. Thoughts—"The beliefs we hold about ourselves, others, and the world, as well as the thought patterns we hold on a day-to-day basis."
3. Imagery—"What we choose to imagine and what our subconscious mind is generating—the subconscious mind works in images, which are dictated by the movies we watch, the books we read, and the experiences we subject ourselves to that go into our memory."

Chapter 7

Confidence

You are very powerful, provided you know how powerful you are.

—YOGI BHAJAN, SPIRITUAL LEADER
AND ENTREPRENEUR

Many people worship celebrities and their fame. It's super-easy to get caught up thinking that your role model is better than you. That they can do all these great things, while you . . . well . . . you are just you . . . *they* are *special.*

You've probably heard of the rapper and performing artist Shawn Carter (also known as Jay-Z). Some people like him and some don't. Regardless of your opinion about his lifestyle, message, and work, he has a remarkably inspiring story. He went from living in the projects in New York to being on the cover of *Forbes* magazine and selling hundreds of millions of hip-hop records. Isn't that just wild? He is a great example of the possibilities we have to create anything we can imagine. Let's put aside whether we agree or disagree with his messages, lyrics, and all that—this is a dude who had nothing and made something. He made his dreams a reality. He did this against all odds with no money and no support. All he had was his dream. Well, a dream, and one other thing. . . .

I knew intuitively there had to have been something else to his success and the difference he's made. Most people have dreams. Then, something happens and they end up becoming old and bitter, focusing on all the bad stuff that happens in life. Jay-Z is definitely not one of those people. He followed his *big* dreams.

So with this in mind I asked myself, what makes Jay-Z so great? What made him able to make his dream a reality? I studied up on him. I searched the Internet for "Jay-Z quotes" and read every one of his quotes off of every website I could find. I read about his success, his life, and his opinions. I found it all very interesting, but none of it spoke about what makes Jay-Z, Jay-Z. What made this guy one of the most influential people of the twenty-first century?

Then I scoured YouTube for hours and watched endless interviews with him. I listened closely and took notes every time he said something I liked. Still, none of what he said was *it*. Finally, somewhere within the hours of YouTube videos I watched, I heard someone in an interview say something like, "Why you? Why did you get to experience this success?" Jay-Z's response was something along the lines of, "Because I look at Leonardo da Vinci and I believe that I am just as great and capable of just as much. I look at Picasso and see myself as a modern-day version. No one does that today. . . . That's why I am me."

When I heard him say that, I thought to myself, *Duh. That's* it. *That's why Jay-Z is where he is.* He has enough *courage* to believe that he is one of the greatest artists to have ever lived. He truly believes that. Whether or not it's true is up to endless interpretation. But what's for sure is that this dude has set a zillion records for album sales, owns nine professional sports teams, and has given more money to charity than most people will ever make in their lives (among a lot of other things).

In a world where most of us idolize greatness, we often forget to ask the question "How? How did the person do it?" If God gave me the quill and ink, and the audacity to write the rules of life, I would say that Jay-Z has been able to accomplish what he has because he saw himself in the same image as his heroes, as one of the greatest artists of all time. He didn't see himself as separate or as less. But please don't get mixed up about this; of course there are a lot of people who are lost in their minds, thinking that they are great, but with nothing to actually prove it. The difference with Jay-Z, however, is that he believes he's the greatest, a living icon, and he proceeds to act as if it is so. He does the work that he feels is required for that to become a reality that the rest of the world sees. He sees eye to eye with the greatest artists of all time, while most people only look in those eyes thinking that the other sees nothing in them. Most people simply look at Picasso's paintings with awe, wondering how he painted such incredible work, while Jay-Z *believes* that he is capable of creating things that are just as great. *Greats aren't great because they were born great, but because they see aspects of themselves in those whom others are saying are great.*

Take Action

Simply telling yourself and others that you're as capable as the greats who have come before you won't get you there. You need to be quiet and work hard to improve your life. Don't just hold an ignorant belief about yourself—let your work speak for you.

This is not quantum physics or rocket science; if you want something you have to go and get it. You have to take action. If you take action, you'll be closer to where you want to be, who you want to become, and what you want to achieve. The only way to take action is by taking action. There's no institution, religion, or five-step process that you must become a part of or become familiar with in order for you to take action. Do what you know you need to do to make it happen. Perhaps you need to read more, learn more, wake up earlier, simply do whatever you need to do to move closer to your goals. Do whatever it is that's going to help you rise to the challenge. It doesn't matter what it is, just start doing it.

It's also always helpful to think about your intentions. Think about all the reasons why you're doing what you're doing, why you want to do it, and why it's important to you. If they're good reasons, you should fight for what you want and what you believe in. A wise man once said, "If you don't stand for something, you fall for everything." If you don't take action when you can, you're going to be stationary your whole life. You're going to miss the sights, sounds, the adventure, and the beautiful struggle. You're going to miss the rewards of feeling satisfied with and proud of yourself. So take action now.

See It Before Anything Happens

In rock star Neil Young's autobiography, *Waging Heavy Peace*, he says that one of the keys to creating great things is that you have to see them before they have happened. The rational mind of our Western world will think *how can you see it before it's happened? I'll believe it when it has actually happened.* But it's so easy to see it before it's happened if we stop looking outside ourselves. The key is *imagination.*

You must feel the vision of something tangibly, even though all you have to show for it is an intangible dream in your hand.

Unfortunately, the voice of the collective consciousness of society says, "But it's hard to use my imagination." If you feel this way, Young reminds us that we must "Be great or be gone." Be the best you can be or get out of the way. See your dream, see your own vision, and feel it before it exists. Then, after you've seen it within, you are prepared to create it in the world.

This was the strategy that Young used. He recalls "being in it for the long haul" when other musicians in his bands quit to get "real jobs." Young is one of the most famous singer/songwriters of all time, and at one point he was so broke that he had to eat Spam and Ritz crackers. He can recall how awful it was not to have any blankets on cold nights. However, despite all of this, he never quit. He felt the vision within him, and nothing and no one could stop him. And eventually, even while struggling to simply feed himself every day, he made it big, and all by the time he was only twenty-four years old.

Neil Young's ability to live his dream was possible because he was passionate and did what he loved to do from a young age. The more you do, the more you develop your dream. Once you have a dream (and you'll know when you do), never settle until you feel it, then see your dream in your imagination, and stick to it for "the long haul," as Young says. You'll live the best life you could have ever imagined. But first, you must . . . see it before anything happens.

Act As If

Nothing ever becomes real until it is experienced.

—John Keats, English Romantic poet

The mind knows no difference between what is and isn't real. If the mind thinks it's experiencing something, especially if you allow yourself to feel it with passion and belief, it doesn't matter if it doesn't seem real to those around you—it will become real if you believe it enough. Imagination is the birthplace of all things.

This is how all things have been created: cars and buildings—they were all initially imagined by their creators. Imagination truly is the birthplace of all things, yet we've been conditioned to think that it's some mystical realm that plays little into the everyday reality of our life. Nothing could be further from the truth. Imagination is the bridge that ushers in new realities. This is why it's so important to act *as if. Act as if* the vision you see within yourself is already a reality, even if circumstance, people, your mind, and your fears, tell you otherwise.

Ever since I was a freshman in college I wanted to be a published author. I wanted to be one of the voices that inspire people around the world. I wanted to prove that, when you follow your dreams and take the adventure of the road less traveled, miracles happen and amazingness unfolds. So after I dropped out of college, quit basketball, and traveled the world, I decided I wanted to write my first book, *Into the Wind*.

I didn't have a clue, at the time, that it's extremely difficult for a first-time author to get a publishing contract for a nonfiction inspirational book. It's more or less impossible—at least that's what everyone told me. My goal was for my favorite publishing company to publish my book. When they denied me and told me to self-publish it, I became furious. (I am hoping that my ability to get so mad fades with age and is just a product of my passion.) I told my agent that this publishing company was going to regret it. We couldn't get a traditional publishing contract, so I published the book myself. I haven't told anyone that until now. People would ask me who my publisher was and I told them. I did have a publisher, but I had to publish the book with my own money. But I didn't tell anyone, not even my parents. I had it imprinted upon my subconscious mind that I was going to sell those books and become a bestselling author. I would sell just as many books as top traditional authors, regardless of how I published my book. Nobody believed in me; even my agent suggested that I lower the sales projections in my book proposal for *Into the Wind*. I agreed, in order to make him happy, but I did not change the integrity of my vision.

Time and time again we see that people who have started from the bottom have made something worthwhile of their lives. I am sitting here today with my second book published by the world's largest publishing company. People ask me how I made this happen, and I tell them that this is what's happening because I proceeded *as if*. I proceeded as if this book would launch my career, and believed that my message would reach countless people around the world. Thinking with this type of surefire belief is what it takes.

Many people call me hardheaded; they say, "That's just Jake, Jake's naive, Jake doesn't know anything about publishing." But I don't need to know anything about publishing. You don't need to know everything about how something's going to work out. You don't need to be an expert. All you need to know is what you want, how you're going to get it, and then never quit. People either quit just before they get to the goal or they make it.

Mark Twain said, "You need two things in life in order to be successful. Confidence and ignorance." I don't believe anything could be truer. Most books don't even sell a few thousand copies. Most books that are published don't really reach anyone. And most authors' self-talk is, "Well, it's really hard to publish books." But the reality is that any field, no matter what it is that you love to do, is competitive. And not only is it competitive, but it's also challenging.

What you must do is *act as if* it has already happened. Nobody knew it, but I told my agent all the time, "I am a bestselling author, I'm gonna make it as an author." His reply was, "Well, let's begin by trying to sell ten books." I tried my best not to be insulted by this when I knew what my vision was, and when I knew what the possibilities were. But it doesn't matter what other people tell you. You must know what the possibilities are, and proceed, even if no one believes you yet. Walk tall, stand tall, and firm up—be who you want to be in five years. That's what it means to *act as if.*

If you hold a vision within yourself long enough, two things can happen: either you eventually give up or you start talking to yourself about how it's not happening. "Well, this isn't happening yet and that's not happening yet." And then you start to no longer *act as if.* You start to act as if it wasn't. And when you act as if it wasn't, that's when the mind shows you that it's not—that your vision is not a reality. But when you can *act as if,* and truly believe that if you continue to take the steps that the way will be made for you, then everything opens up for you.

I remember being devastated when the publishing company of my dreams said "no" to my first book. I had a dream and it didn't become a reality. But when things don't fall into place, it's an opportunity for you either to regress and quit or to strengthen your resolve and open up to the possibility of something even better than what you had previously envisioned. And the only way to proceed toward that possibility is to continue to *act as if their dream has come true,* to live from that space within you. If you believe something long enough, it will become a reality.

Jim Carrey and Visualization

When I was very young I visualized myself being and having
what it was I wanted. Mentally I never had any doubts about
it. The mind is really so incredible. Before I won my first Mr.
Universe title, I walked around the tournament like I owned
it. The title was already mine. I had won it so many times in
my mind that there was no doubt I would win it. Then when
I moved on to the movies, the same thing. I visualized myself
being a famous actor and earning big money. I could feel and
taste success. I just knew it would all happen.

—Arnold Schwarzenegger

Every night, Jim Carrey, the famous blockbuster actor and advo-
cate of living an empowered life, used to drive to Mulholland
Drive and visualize his success. This was around 1986, when he
was flat broke—he literally had nothing and was not getting any
jobs as an actor. He would go to Mulholland Drive and sit, visual-
izing what his life would look like if he was a successful actor with
big directors and producers calling him, letting him know how
much they loved his work. He would sit there and fully go into his
imagination, dreaming about his fantasy, and seeing his life. He
imagined the best possible version of life, the one he wanted to
live. He'd see it all, and feel it all—he allowed himself to experience it in his imagination.

When he would drive home, his life wasn't actually the way he
was imagining it (yet), but he would visualize the fantasy with such
persistence and commitment that he would drive home thinking,
"Well, I am living my dream. I am living this life. I have everything I am dreaming of, it's just not exactly happening yet." Then

one day, he wrote a check for $10 million, for acting services rendered. He gave himself three or four years to achieve it and dated it Thanksgiving 1995. That was when he imagined that the check would be valid. He kept the check in his wallet all the time. It started deteriorating over time and it would go into his mind every time he saw it. Then, just before Thanksgiving 1995, he found out he was going to make $10 million for *Dumb and Dumber.*

"Visualization works if you work hard," Carrey says. "But you can't just visualize and then go eat a sandwich." You've got to think of your belief system in a practical way. You've got to see it first—the more you see it, the more you believe it. And the more you see and believe it, the more action you will take to make it a reality.

However, you must keep in mind that just because you write the check, or visualize what you want, it doesn't mean you are automatically going to get it. A lot of people visualize, but don't actually put forward motion in the direction of their dreams. You cannot only think about what you want, you must also take steps toward it—you must *do.* Also, even if you think you know very clearly what it is that you want, you need to allow yourself to stay open to even greater possibilities. Your dream may be a pre-dream to something even bigger and more suited for you and your specific gifts. The most important thing is to keep moving forward toward the dream even if things are not working exactly to plan—do not give up.

Many people resist believing in their dreams and working toward them because the current circumstances of their lives aren't compatible with the ones they are trying to move toward—or who they are today is not who they are trying to become. They see their self-defeating habits, realize that they aren't fully living in integrity, or don't believe that they are the type of person who can have what they want, live their dreams, or make a difference. And because they think this way, their subconscious mind resists creating their dreams.

Regardless of whether or not you believe in yourself, your dreams will not become a reality overnight. You may begin to see little signs that your dream is a possibility when you feel clear about what you want, but things take time. There's a process that needs to happen, which is only expedited and brought to fruition when you work hard and keep taking steps in the direction of your goal.

Getting what you want isn't a mystical mystery—it begins with knowing what you want and taking action. You must know that just because you don't get what you want right away doesn't mean you aren't going to get it in time. You will arrive where you want to go if you continue forward. In life, it's true that you don't get what you want, but you do get to be who you believe you are, who you believe you are capable of becoming. When you live life from this space, with this type of thinking, you can overcome any challenges you face.

When publishers told me they weren't going to publish my first book, I could have quit. I could have become angry or pessimistic. But instead I thought, *well, something greater is opening up for me as an author*, and I stayed open to that possibility. Then, not even a year later, the biggest publishing company in the world is publishing the book you are reading.

Remember, if you run into challenges and don't get exactly what you want, it's because something greater is coming your way. If you stay focused and connected to your vision (with a positive mind-set), believing, feeling, and seeing what you want, nothing can take it away from you. If and when you get stuck, think about Jim Carrey—remember that he was flat broke, but didn't let his circumstances take his dream away. He kept moving forward, which is exactly what you and I must do.

Just Start, No Matter What

You don't have to be good to start . . . you just have to start to
be good!

—Joe Sabah, speaker, trainer, consultant, author, and publisher

In 1966, a dyslexic sixteen-year-old boy dropped out of school.
Shortly thereafter, he started a magazine for students. He had only
a little bit of money to get started, so he sold advertisements in the
magazine to businesses and ran the operation out of a local church.
He didn't groan about his lack of resources or qualifications. Instead of thinking about what he didn't have, he took advantage of
what he did have.

Only a few years later, he started selling mail-order records to
students who bought the magazine. The records started selling
really well, so he built his first record store the next year. Then, a
couple of years later, he started a record label and built recording
studios, which he rented out to artists. Eventually, the first song
ever recorded in his studios sold five million copies, and over the
next decade the kid grew his record label by adding bands like the
Sex Pistols and the Rolling Stones.

Throughout the whole process, this person never stopped
creating new ideas and new companies. He never gave up on his
incredible vision for his life. He has not only started an airline
business and a mobile phone company, but within fifty years he has
built four hundred more companies. That kid who dropped out of
school stayed focused, persistent, and creative despite his "learning
disabilities," "inexperience," and "lack of knowledge"—and today
he is a billionaire who has changed the way the world conducts
business. His name is Sir Richard Branson. He is the founder of

the Virgin Group. He named his enterprise Virgin because he started with zero experience or qualifications in business.

Branson accomplished all of this because he didn't give in to the excuses so many of us use to explain why we can't succeed. Instead, he followed what he is famously quoted for: "Screw it. Just do it." Just take action and the way will be made for you. Just allow yourself to figure it out along the way, while on the path. You simply need to get started, to take the first steps. No one is qualified for anything, and you will never actually be ready. If you wish to live the highest quality of life you can, you need to go beyond fear, and the only way to do so is by trying. You need to dream big and believe in yourself—just like Richard Branson.

You may think that you have a good reason, a rational one, as to why you aren't ready to take the next leap in your life. But no matter what that leap is, whether it's reaching out to a stranger you find attractive, starting a new company, writing a book, recording an album, building a house, going back to school, or traveling, you are never going to feel completely ready. You are never going to have the solution for every potential failure. You're never going to know everything. And, frankly, you don't want to know everything. If you did, the fun and uncertainty would be taken out of life. The freedom you feel from the excitement of not knowing would be gone. So just get going and figure it out on the fly.

You may have excuses that want to hold you back from making your dreams a reality, but you can still do it, you can still help people, and you can still find your purpose. One could argue that Branson isn't qualified for what he's doing with his life, but it doesn't matter—he's doing it. Belief in yourself is enough to get you beyond your excuses. Don't think rationally about any of this. Don't try to justify why you're not ready to take that step. You'll never feel ready enough. Just start now.

Mozhdah Jamalzadah

Mozhdah Jamalzadah, Afghan-Canadian singer and model, was five years old the first time she heard the sound of rockets flying over her head. That was when she thought that the whole world was at war, when she believed that every child on earth couldn't play on their playgrounds without the threat of being blown up by rockets and missiles. She was living in Afghanistan at the time, and when she was six her family fled the country, driving through the mountains in a little beat-up truck, to live as refugees in Pakistan.

Eventually, she moved to Canada and, while growing up there, she started to take an interest in what was happening back in Afghanistan. She wanted to find a way to help women there because they have very few rights. She couldn't stand hearing stories about Afghan women who were being stoned to death for "committing adultery."

When interviewed about this time of her life, she says, "Well, I thought I'd grow up to be a lawyer and help the people who were being taken advantage of. My mom always told me that I had great opportunities to make a difference and that I needed to pursue them. I took that to heart. I was a book nerd and pretty much knew nothing about music." She may not have known anything about music, but she did know that there were many songs on the radio, and that many people heard those songs all around the world. She felt that becoming a musician would be a way to make a difference and have her voice and message heard in a big way. She took singing lessons for three years, started making music, and eventually became famous in Afghanistan. Her career was taking off and she was given her own television show. The show was modeled after *Oprah*, but for people in Afghanistan.

At this time she was hearing more about all the terrible things that were happening to women in Afghanistan and she became increasingly more upset. One day, just before she was set to film one of the episodes of her show, she heard that a woman tried to set herself on fire and failed, twice. When the woman was asked what she would have done differently the next time, she said, "Well, I would try to get a gun." This really affected Jamalzadah, so she started speaking out on her television show against oppression and for women's rights.

At the end of the show's season, Jamalzadah received a phone call from her manager, who very worriedly asked where she was. He called because there was a rumor circulating around Afghanistan that Jamalzadah had been killed. People were saying that her nose and ears had been cut off and her head severed to show women that they should not speak out for women's rights. Her manager told her that she could not go back to Afghanistan. At the time, she was in Europe. She decided to go back to Afghanistan anyway.

When she arrived, she received calls from government officials every day, including the chief of police of Kabul. The chief of police was actually calling for her safety, telling her to leave. The situation started to get really bad, so she had to go into hiding at her uncle's house and was forced to leave the country a few days after her family packed up her stuff.

She went back to Canada, but she is not giving up. She wants to have a show again, and wants to speak for all the people who are being oppressed. She wants to help people in her country, and those in other countries, who are being taken advantage of. Her mom encourages her by saying, "Well, you know, if they forced you out of the country and they've turned your life into this, why not do it again in an even bigger way? Make a bigger voice. Make more trouble for them, to help more people." Now Jamalzadah wants to bring her voice to America so she can have a bigger platform. She says, "I've set new goals and I'm never going to give up because I'm here to make a difference."

No matter what you think your excuse is, whether it's the country you're from, your lack of resources, your being plagued by your past, or your gender, don't let fear limit the size of your dream. If you want to help people, you'll figure out a way to get past your fear. Step out of the false story that you're not qualified, not ready, and not capable of taking the next big step in your life.

Age Does Not Matter

Life has no pause buttons; dreams have no expiry date; time has no holiday, so don't miss a single moment in your life.

—Ritu Ghatourey, Indian author

Someone once told me that age has no license on wisdom. And I would add that age has no license on intelligence, no license on potential, and no license on possibilities. If you believe in what you're doing, and are doing what you're meant to do, age has no effect on the life you are capable of living.

Age is one of life's most misunderstood concepts. We are often trained to believe that our life is like climbing a mountain—we start at the bottom, learning to walk when we're young, and we reach the peak of the mountain, the pinnacle of our life, when we're in our best shape, somewhere around our mid-twenties. That is when we're supposed to be at our most vital, with our minds and bodies working best. That is supposed to be the peak in our lives. Then you stay up around the peak, and then somewhere around fifty, you start to get older. You're not *old* yet, but you're getting older. Then, when you approach your sixties, seventies, and eight-ies, people tell you that you are old, and you start to slow down. You think of yourself in terms of different possibilities, potential, and capabilities.

Dreams have no expiration dates, and neither does the human spirit. Manifest the image that you hold of yourself; you're simply a reflection of your own imagination. The famous comedian Bill Hicks explains that if you're going to hold an image of yourself, it should be an empowering one.

I'll never forget what Laird Hamilton said to me when I inter-viewed him: "Somebody always has it worse than you. And some-body always has it better than you, so you can always do something and be humble at the same time." When I reflect on that today, some years later, I realize that it also applies to age. Belief systems are often linked to age. People think they can or cannot do things because of how old they are. When we were young, we were told we were too little, and when we are old, we are told we are too old. But we're never too young or too old, to do whatever it is that we want to do. People have done beautiful, exciting, wildly successful, fun things, and have made a huge difference in the world, at all ages. You can find examples all throughout human history.

Bucky Lasek

Bucky Lasek is the world's most successful vert skateboarder. Looking at his career and accomplishments makes me think that he's one of the most successful and historic skateboarders who have ever lived, and I have uncovered one of the secrets to his success— he doesn't look at age in a limiting way.

He sat down with me shortly after he swept all four golds in vert skating in the X Games in 2013.

He won the gold in every single competition for the year, which is historic and absolutely incredible. Once in Los Angeles, once in Munich, once in Barcelona, and lastly in Brazil! It's also noteworthy that he's forty-two years old and was in this competition with people half his age.

"Usually, when we turn forty-two, we think 'That's pretty old,'" I said. "How do you go beyond that?"

He scoffed when I mentioned his age. I smiled too. "It doesn't matter," he said in such a simple and practical way. It made it so easy to uncover why Bucky Lasek is Bucky Lasek.

"If I want to do something, then I'll just do it. I don't need excuses. I want to be the best I can be. Period," he explained.

Bucky is one of the most incredible athletes alive in the twenty-first century, despite the fact that he is in his forties. That's because he sets up belief systems that empower him, and believes that his passion alone is the most important thing. He wants to be the best that he can be and knows that he can regardless of his age. During his career, he has experienced success in times that people see him as young and old.

Bucky taught me that he holds a high standard of greatness for himself. It's something he will never give up. He also explained that his standard for greatness is determined by his love for what he does, not by the made-up number that explains the state of his body.

Hearing wisdom like this is exactly why we must ask ourselves "how" when we see someone with a lot of potential or achieving a high level of success. Finding the "how" allows us to see ourselves in Bucky Lasek, or in the person we pass by on the street. When we see someone's smile, we must walk over, get to know them, and find out what makes them happy. Seeing ourselves in others and asking "how" helps us learn.

Gabe Eggerling

I met and interviewed ten-year-old Gabe Eggerling. Eggerling is a boy who has donated more than two thousand books to kids who don't have any money and can't buy books. He's done this for kids that live in places ranging from Southern California to Guatemala. I met him because we both gave a TED talk the same night. He was wearing a Superman costume, and his talk was on how superheroes are ordinary people just like us. Or rather, extraordinary people just like us.

Every week, Eggerling receives drawings, pictures, and thank-you letters from kids who have received his books. He's been featured in books with presidents of the United States for the incredible things he's accomplished. Remember, he is ten years old. I asked him about overcoming the fear of being too young. He said, "It doesn't matter how old you are." He went on to explain that age is just a number, that age isn't real. He said, "As long as you believe in yourself, as long as you're creative, and as long as you are yourself, you can achieve anything. It doesn't matter how old you are. And it doesn't matter how young you are."

Eggerling started helping thousands of people when he was just seven years old. But just because he is an incredible young man doesn't mean that he doesn't face challenges. He's had people tell him time and again that he's too young, that he should go sit at a kiddie table, or that he needs to wait ten or twenty years before he can really make a difference. He's also been denied numerous projects. I asked him how that made him feel. He replied, "It hurts! It really hurts me. The most important thing isn't how old you are, it's how you act, it's how strong you are, and how responsible you are. It's not how many numbers you are, because numbers aren't real. I've been doing what I've been doing for three years, so that proves that age isn't important. If you have an arm, a leg, two lungs, and your toes, that's all that matters. None of your excuses are legitimate, and even if you don't have any of that, even if you're missing an arm or a leg, you can still do it, because you have a heart, you have a spirit, and you have determination inside of you—even if you haven't accessed it yet. You're gonna face challenges, but look for the solutions."

When Eggerling ran out of funding to help kids around the world, he found partners. He looked at his problem, which was a lack of resources, and solved it. This is a great example, because lack of resources is a problem that many of us encounter. Whether it's not having enough money, not having enough people to sell a product to, not having a house, or not having courage, most of us have experienced this problem. We must stop thinking about this problem and look for the solution like Eggerling did. You may not get everything you need right away, but you can probably get something that will help you continue on.

You're not too young and you're not too old; you're perfect just the way you are. Remember that you have everything you need in order to take the steps. Believe in yourself! Be creative and be yourself. You can make a difference whether you are ten years old or 100 years old. You can live the way you want to live, and you can still do all the things you want to do.

I asked Eggerling when he realized that he wanted to make a difference. He explained that when he was about five years old he realized that the purpose of life was to make a difference. I asked him how he knew that. He replied, "Because it feels good, and I wanna feel good about my life."

If you wanna feel good about your life, if you wanna feel good about yourself, don't let age limit you. You don't need to let age limit you—it's just a number. It's not real. You have a heart and you have an imagination, so use them! You're gonna face challenges, everyone does, but don't let a number limit you. You are much more than a number.

If You Don't Know
Who You Are . . .

People often ask me, "How do you take action and start to live the life you want if you don't know who you are?" One time, after one of my speeches, somebody asked me this, and added, "And who are you, Jake?" I replied, "Well, I don't really know who I am and I don't need to know exactly who I am. I only need to know what I want and how I can start taking action to get it."

You are never going to know exactly who you are, because your identity is endless—it changes and grows every day. You are an infinite stream of potential, so trying to know every aspect of yourself is limiting. However, through experience, experimentation, trying new things, taking risks, and facing challenges, you will uncover more of who you are. You will find out more about what you like and what you don't like. With this type of discovery, you can make better-informed choices that enhance your life. You must simply observe your habits, your reactions, what you like, what you don't like, and how you act. This doesn't mean, however, that you will ever know exactly who you are. Besides, we are constantly changing—this is part of the beauty of life. And knowing exactly who you are takes away the mystery about you and what you came here to do.

Yes, you're a beautiful mystery. You're rapture. One of the beautiful aspects of life is our ability to put ourselves in different kinds of situations. Each time you encounter a unique situation, you find out more about yourself—you find thoughts, emotions, and truths that you didn't even know existed inside of you.

You don't need to know exactly who you are. All you need to know is what you want to feel. If it's freedom, then start doing things that make you feel free. If it's joy, start to do things that make you feel joyous. It's that simple. Find out what you want to experience in life and start taking action. Uncovering who you are happens along the way. And again, I stress the fact that you'll never truly know everything about who you are. I don't know everything about who I am, and yet, I do know what I am capable of—I know my preferences, and I know how to begin taking action.

Chapter 8

Persistence

> *Nothing in this world can take the place of persistence. Talent will not: nothing is more common than unsuccessful men with talent. Genius will not: unrewarded genius is almost a proverb. Education will not: the world is full of educated derelicts. Persistence and determination alone are omnipotent.*
>
> —CALVIN COOLIDGE

You've got to be hungry for something more from your life. You've got to be scrappy. You've got to hustle. This is what makes or breaks the quality of your life.

Dave Matthews of the Dave Matthews Band wasn't always the world's most successful live musician. At one point, he couldn't even get a record contract or get his albums into stores. The only thing he knew was what he wanted. He traveled with his band around America in a sedan. They slept on couches and floors, played in houses and backyards, and sold over 100,000 albums out

of the trunk of their car before they established themselves as serious musicians.

He reached his current level of success because he didn't give
up. He was persistent, creative, and focused on the end result,
which was to tour around the world and fill arenas—to inspire
people through music.

You must be persistent in what you love. Bob Marley is another great example. Today, T-shirts with Bob's face on them are
the highest-selling public-figure T-shirts in the world. But, Bob
was not always this popular. He grew up in Trenchtown, where
people were so hungry that an inside joke with the kids in his
neighborhood was, "Drink some water and go to bed. Fill your
stomach up with water and go to bed." Trenchtown was one of the
poorest places in all of Jamaica.

Despite the poverty that Bob Marley grew up with, he saw a
way out—music. He pounded the pavement and worked hard.
However, when he and the Wailers finally produced an album,
they didn't get any recognition. When things don't go the way we
want them to, we often give up, but Bob Marley knew that we are
not entitled to anything in the world. We have to go out and get it.

Bob Marley said, "If you don't start somewhere, you're never
gonna get nowhere." So Bob Marley and the Wailers started playing free concerts all around Jamaica. They were still making no
money, but they were getting their sound out there. Eventually,
they borrowed money to buy a car and then they went by car to
every radio station in the country doing this day after day, all day
long. They started going door to door, to literally *every* radio station in Jamaica, with their albums, saying, "Play this. Play this
music." If the radio station said no, Marley and his group sat there
until the radio station played the songs. They were so convinced

that everything would work out that they proceeded as if this method would work for sure. They were persistent.

They ended up with a number-one hit single. They became some of the most successful musicians in Jamaica. But that wasn't where Marley's vision ended. His vision was to bring together not just Jamaica with his music, but the whole world. He wanted to reach the entire Western world.

They signed a contract with Chris Blackwell and Island Records. Chris Blackwell told them, "If you want to be successful, you have to go on a year-long tour, a promotion tour, which means you're going to make no money." His group headed out to Europe, and at this time nobody knew who they were. No one had ever heard of them. And you have to imagine the scene: they're from Jamaica, and at the time it was the middle of winter in Europe. They were touring around in the freezing cold with no budget, and no financial compensation. And they knew they'd have to do that for a year to build momentum.

This ended up being too much for most of the band members, so many of them quit. But Marley knew that he had to do it. He kept motivated with his mantra, "If you don't start somewhere, you're never gonna get nowhere." He continued to travel around in a sedan in the freezing cold, oftentimes feeling miserable, eating bad food, and getting no sleep. But he kept going, he kept committing to it, and he kept moving forward.

After that year, Marley made little to no progress financially, but he was developing his skills and strengthening as a result. At the end, Bob Marley and the Wailers were launched. They were known all around the Western world.

But this still wasn't where Marley wanted to stop. His goal was to bring people together and grow and grow and grow. As he became famous and wealthy, he was so committed to bringing peace around the world that he spent his own money to play free concerts. He even flew his equipment out to Africa and put on free concerts there.

One night, Marley held one of the largest concerts in Jamaican history, Smile Jamaica—hundreds of thousands of Jamaicans showed up. One important detail about this concert is that Marley was shot the night before the concert. He literally had a bullet go into his body and was almost killed—yet he was so committed to what he was doing that he went out the next night, twelve hours later, and performed the concert.

Marley made choices such as these because he was committed to what he was doing. He was persistent and believed in his mission. A few years later Marley was diagnosed with cancer, but he continued to tour around the world. He only stopped when his body failed him and he collapsed. Now that's persistence.

Being great involves never giving up. It's never compromising on your dreams. It's making no excuses. It's being persistent. There is nothing in the world that can replace persistence.

Some people think that Bob Marley did what he did because he was just some crazy, pot-smoking hippie. But Roger Steffens, who traveled on tour with Marley and has written dozens of books about him, explains the truth about these misconceptions: "There are dozens of misconceptions about Bob. People think he was just a stoned-out freak who was smoking dope all the time. On the contrary, I think he was one of the most disciplined human beings I've ever met in my life. I spent two weeks on the road with him in '79 on his Survival tour. He was always the first guy on the bus and the last guy to go to bed at night and the first guy to wake up in the morning. He probably only slept three or four hours a night and just wanted everything to be absolutely professional and perfect."

Twilight

The Twilight series was a megahit, both in movie theaters and in bookstores. However, the story was formally rejected by nine literary agencies before creator Stephenie Meyer found an agent to sell her manuscript. She finished the manuscript in three months and wrote to fifteen agencies soon after. Eventually, one gave her a chance. Then, eight publishers auctioned for the right to publish *Twilight*. At the time, Meyer received a three-book deal worth $750,000. Her net worth now exceeds $40 million.

While we may only see the bright and shiny lights of success from many projects and people, it's never an easy road to get there. The path to reaching your dreams is filled with torment, despair, and self-doubt. So when you encounter these feelings, you need to be persistent. You need the will to overcome whatever is blocking your way. You need to know that if it were too easy, it wouldn't be worth it, and that if you give up, you're proving that you do not deserve it.

When I start making excuses for why my dreams won't come true, I always remind myself of these words from Bernard Schaffer, police detective, author, and former child actor: "Listen, Stephen King used to write in the washroom of his trailer after his kids went to sleep. Elmore Leonard got up at 5:00 a.m. every morning to write before work. Every time my alarm goes off at 5:00 a.m. and I don't want to get up, or would rather play video games, I think about those guys. Stop screwing around and finish your damn book."

Although Schaffer may be speaking about authors, the message is universal: the great influencers of the world never settled for mediocre effort. If you want something bad enough, you will be persistent enough to make it happen.

Hard Work

Of course there has to be some talent involved, but talent is a dreadfully cheap commodity, cheaper than table salt. What separates the talented individual from the successful one is a lot of hard work and study; a constant process of honing.

—Stephen King

Hard work is doing something even when you feel like doing something else—again, and again, and again. Hard work means you must *keep coming back*. Again in the morning when you're tired. Again in the afternoon when you feel like just hanging out. Again in the evening before you go to bed.

Hard work is the discipline of prolonged focus on an intention created by the mind. It's the ultimate superpower. Hard work means knowing that you're tired, and feeling like you can't go another day, but going another day anyway. You keep showing up, and you keep putting your heart and your soul into your life. You keep putting your heart and your soul into other people, and into your talents.

Hard work is the ability to discern what's most important in life and then doing that thing with the utmost enthusiasm. Not for fifteen minutes, an hour, a day, or a weekend. It's doing it each and every day. It's having a standard of greatness and believing that you are capable of doing a lot.

When you feel that you've hit a wall or hit your edge, you'll fall down, but then you'll get back up again. Again and again, you must show up with a smile on your face and gratitude in your heart for the opportunity to keep moving forward. Keep your mind focused on the opportunity, on the possibility, on the intention, on your values, and on knowing that you cannot compromise on any of these. You must show up every day with tenacity. You cannot be complacent and passive. You must be firm, strong, enthusiastic, and disciplined. You have to be there. You have to be here.

Abe Lincoln

> The most interesting thing about a postage stamp is the persistence with which it sticks to its job.
>
> —Napoleon Hill, author in the area of the New Thought movement,
> and American business magnate Andrew Carnegie's apprentice

How many times have we stopped doing what we were born to do? We often blame it on our intelligence, our physical strength, our talent, bad timing, or on the lack of money we have. Abraham Lincoln could have used all of these excuses, and more.

Born into poverty, Lincoln had to struggle immensely to get into politics. And this was not too long after the defeat he faced as a child, which could've been the perfect excuse to believe that he couldn't change the world. His family was so poor that they were evicted from their home, and as a child Abe had to work to help support them. His mother also died while he was young, so he didn't have her support. Lincoln continued to work hard while growing up, but went bankrupt, and spent seventeen years of his life paying off his debts.

During this process of hard work and persistence, Lincoln started to run for state legislature and lost eight times. Around the same time, Lincoln was engaged and his fiancée died. The combination of the loss and the death caused him to suffer a nervous breakdown that left him bedridden for six months.

After he recovered, he tried to become a speaker for state legislature, but lost. He also tried to become an elector, but lost again. Then, he ran for Congress and lost. Then, he ran again, and this time he *finally* won. Soon after, he ran for reelection but lost. Then he ran for land officer in his home state of Kentucky, but was rejected. Then, he lost the election for the United States Senate. Next, he was slightly humiliated when seeking the vice presidential nomination, and received fewer than one hundred votes. As a result, he ran for Senate again and lost. Then, he was elected for president of the United States of America, and not only did he win, but he is remembered today as one of the best presidents who ever lived.

What does Abe's story show us? That we must grind until the rough is smooth, and the smooth is smoother. If you continue to get up, you will eventually find out who you really are, and what you're really made of. Your character is determined by what you do during the sixth, and seventh, setback. Author Greg Kincaid says it best: "No matter how much falls on us, we keep plowing ahead. That's the only way to keep the roads clear."

Life isn't magical all the time, and even if it is, it's not sweet like roses all the time. You're not the only one who wants to give up, and feels like you aren't good enough. Let Abraham Lincoln's story show you that there are things truly worth living for. And the best part is that you never know when you'll find these things. You just need to keep going forward.

Dig Deep

Man is a stream whose source is hidden.

—Ralph Waldo Emerson, American essayist, lecturer, and poet

You don't know how strong you are until you have no choice but to be strong. When your back is against the wall, you conjure up more capabilities, more strength, more creativity, and more courage than you ever thought possible. This is what it means to dig deep and go beyond yourself—you have to let go of who you think you are and what you think you're capable of, and draw upon something greater. The more opportunities we give ourselves to test our inner strength, the more we can live from this powerful state of being. But you have to go out there and try, otherwise you will only see your power and strength as some random fluke that happens periodically, or only in moments of extreme crisis.

We have no idea who we are and what we are capable of doing. People like Martin Luther King Jr., Gandhi, Anne Frank, and Rosa Parks only tapped into the surface of the well of human potential, and they found it because their backs were against the wall. They found this inner strength because they were in life-and-death situations, where either their lives or the lives of those around them were directly threatened. The threats on their lives ranged from guns to concentration camps, and yet they still drew upon the strength within themselves. They didn't let fear take over. They believed that people didn't deserve to live life with such horrid oppression, so they dug deep to find their inner power.

Van Gogh

Courage is the most important of all the virtues, because without courage you can't practice any other virtue consistently.

—Maya Angelou

Persistence is courage. It's the courage to believe that no matter
how bad it is or how bad it gets, you're still going to make it. By
make it, I don't mean getting to a certain place in space and time,
but traveling through space and time with the courage to do what
you love.

This was what Vincent van Gogh did. He sold only one painting in his entire lifetime! He was so persistent and determined to
do what he loved that he didn't even care if his paintings sold—he
was determined to keep going, no matter what. And do you know
who he sold his one painting to? His friend. But this didn't stop
him. He kept going, and before the end of his life he had com-
pleted over eight hundred paintings.

His work is timeless because he never let anything affect what
he knew he must do. He never let anything stop him from doing
what he loved. And because he believed in himself, everyone wants
to buy his work even today. His most expensive painting is valued
at $142.7 million.

Van Gogh's life teaches us the truth that one of my favorite
musicians, rapper Macklemore, recognizes: "The greats were great
not because at birth they could paint. The greatest were great because they paint a lot." And if this isn't convincing enough, let Van
Gogh's own words help you believe otherwise: "If you hear a voice
within say 'You cannot paint,' then by all means, paint, and that
voice will be silenced."

Persistence Creates Bridges

Imagine your father dies working on the project of his dreams, and then you lose a lot of your brain function in another accident. But you know deep within you that you must keep going! The problem is that you have only one finger that works.

You are so determined and know that persistence is building doors where there seem to be walls. So while recovering in the hospital, you develop a communication system with your wife by using that one finger, signaling to her to contact engineers. Once she did, you again moved your finger slowly but surely for thirteen years in order to communicate with the engineers about how to complete the project!

That's how the Brooklyn Bridge was built, starting in the early 1800s! That determined but injured engineer's father, John Roebling, had a dream to connect Manhattan and Brooklyn. No one thought it was possible—they told him it was unrealistic. They told him to stop because it wasn't safe.

Half a year into the project, Roebling was killed, and his son was injured so severely injured in a separate accident that he couldn't talk or walk. That didn't stop him from using every ounce of willpower he had in order to keep going, despite the challenges. That's what it takes—at least, that's what it took in order to build the Brooklyn Bridge—a "never give up and never give in" attitude.

Let it show you that even when you are faced with physical challenges, even when the unspeakable happens, there may still be a way. In fact, there is always a way, there is always a road, but oftentimes the only way to get there is to disregard every voice that says it's impossible. Odds are one thing, but giving up because they are against you is like the sun deciding not to rise because it's too cloudy and it won't be able to shine as effortlessly as usual.

Inspiration (through Dissatisfaction)

It's natural for us to get down on ourselves when we fail or something doesn't go as planned. Especially when we don't perform the way we know we're capable of performing. Often when this occurs, we become dissatisfied and beat ourselves up about it. We expect ourselves to be perfect.

Human beings are imperfect, so we might as well accept this fact and do our best anyway. Personally, I like to use discontentment with circumstances or myself as inspiration. Oftentimes we think that being discontent with ourselves is not okay. But I invite you to think that if it happens, it happens, and you should use it to your advantage. Anger and frustration can be powerful emotions that spark our creativity and productivity if channeled properly.

Laird Hamilton (world champion big-wave surfer) once told me, "It's not like I don't let things get me down. I am just not accepting that they will become my outcome." Later that night, after interviewing Hamilton, I watched the footage of the interview with him, twice. He was saying that being dissatisfied or not getting what you want is part of life, as is frustration and feeling let down.

When you feel these emotions, you have two choices. The first is getting down on yourself, becoming your own worst critic, engaging in negative self-talk that brings down your self-esteem, and getting mad at yourself for getting upset in the first place. Or you can choose to be like Hamilton, who feels the angst, but channels it to get motivated and take action to get out of the circumstances as best and as fast as he can. Hamilton's use of the energy is much more productive—using the energy to feel negative and doubtful makes it hard to get motivated and change the situation.

W. Clement Stone, businessman, philanthropist, and New Thought self-help book author, taught that *dissatisfied inspiration* is an important principle to use to help you do great things in your life. People who seek more out of life need to be okay with accepting that they may fail, feel cheated, or get off the path for a little while. The big difference, however, between them and the majority of the population is that they don't allow themselves to feel defeated and give up. They know that they are not meant to stay where they don't want to be. Nevertheless, they are not happy-go-lucky all the time. They do get upset, but they use their discontentment as motivation to work harder, get better, and try, as best as they can, not to put themselves in the same situation again.

If you feel dissatisfied at one time or another, or perhaps right now, with one or more areas of your life, use that bitter emotion as fuel to drive you to something more. Recycle your emotions. Put them into the fire of your belly, and let them propel you forward toward a greater quality of life.

You are human. It's okay to feel discontent or out of balance. But don't get stuck there. Feel it, recognize it, and take right action to transcend it. Highly effective people recognize these moments as the opportunity to become something more.

Gold Medalist
(through Discontentment)

"If I mess up, it makes me work harder," skateboarder Bucky Lasek told me. "I just always want to be better than I was. I get pissed at myself and I use that as fuel." Here, Lasek uses the same phil-osophy as Hamilton—he simply expresses it with slightly different words.

Lasek continued by explaining he is often very critical, espe-cially of himself. Many of us are critical, but oftentimes when we find ourselves feeling that way, we mope around, become lazy, and sulk. Lasek, on the other hand, uses this feeling as a tool to push him to reach his potential—there is a drive within him to be the best he can possibly be. He has, like many of us, a high standard for his capabilities. And though he is top in his field in the world, he still fails to meet his expectations at times. The key is that he uses that bitter taste of occasional dissatisfaction to work harder to achieve his goals. I would be curious to see how all of our lives would change if, instead of sulking or feeling bad, we used that stale emotion to propel us forward.

Adaptability

> It is not the strongest of the species that survives, nor the most intelligent that survives. It is the one that is the most adaptable to change.
>
> —Charles Darwin, naturalist
> and geologist

"What's one of the secrets to getting the most out of life?" I asked surfer Rob Machado. His response: "Adaptability." He told me about the constant state of flux that he was in as one of the top competitive surfers in the world. At that time of his life, he trav-eled all around the world with other surfers. Every time they would arrive at a new place, they would have to go out in the water and perform in front of a panel of a few judges who were traveling with them. The judges would then rank the surfers and, based off of the number of their ranking, the surfers' career and possibilities would be determined. The stability of their career, life, and future was based on competing against other people.

Machado explained that there was so much going on and things were always changing. He would get thrown into situations where he didn't have his board, or where he wouldn't have the same board he had been using, and he would have to change boards again. (As a surfer, you become accustomed to certain boards and changing them can really throw you off.) He would then arrive on the other side of the world the next week and the weather would be totally different. It could be stormy and windy, and although he didn't want to go out, it didn't matter—he had to go out. He was put in situations with conditions that he didn't want and at times it would cause a lot of stress. And there were moments when he didn't feel passionate about what he was doing, but he had to go out and do it anyway.

We can all relate to this. In life, we are often faced with situations that we don't want to face, but we have to face them anyway. When life brings us such circumstances, we have to be able to adapt to them. When the waves and storms of life come, we need to stay centered, calm, connected to ourselves, and strong.

You can continue to grow and better yourself by staying focused and adapting. That's one of the keys to everything in life, from business to being one of the greatest surfers in the world, like Rob Machado. Simply adapt to life and its seasons. I am sure each of you can remember a time when you enjoyed a really cold or hot day. It's possible. So even when life gives us extreme situations or temperatures, the key is adapting to them—allowing yourself to adjust, enjoy, and feel pleasure.

From the Ground Up

Jay-Z—you probably love him or hate him. At least, most people do. But the one thing we can't deny is that the dude knows how to reach millions of people, make millions of dollars, and become the face of commercially successful music around the world.

I mean, he's a musician who makes the *Forbes* list, with a net worth of half a billion dollars. And he has hit song after hit song after hit song. But what fascinates me most about the guy is not his fame; fortune; beautiful wife, Beyoncé; or how many albums he's made. It's his persistence that catches my attention!

Many people don't realize that this was a young man who couldn't get a record deal. Every record label rejected his music. But he didn't care—he just took other people's opinions as just that, their opinions.

He believed in himself despite the world telling him no. As a result, he built his own record label, Roc-A-Fella, and began selling CDs out of the trunk of his car and performing in front of whoever would show up! Today he is one of the bestselling musical artists of all time and performs to stadiums full of people!

He created the very dream he had as a child—to get out of the streets of New York and away from the violence with the help of music. All of the odds were stacked against him. No money or college education. No record label. But he once said, "Ain't nothin' wrong with the aim, just gotta change the target."

And how sweet his successes must feel knowing that, when things are going the way you would've hoped, you don't give up, you maybe just need to change your target. You may just need to stop waiting for someone to help you, and do it yourself! You may just need to realize that nothing is impossible unless you give up. You may not be where you want to be today, but you must clench your fist and fight for your dreams, no matter what!

Chapter 9

Consistency

Famous actor Will Smith says that a greatly misunderstood concept is the difference between talent and skill. He says that talent is something that you have naturally, but it's not all you need—your talent will fail you if you aren't skilled. You must spend hours and hours working on your craft.

Smith attributes his success to being skilled. He doesn't view himself as a particularly talented person. He says that he's never been the smartest or naturally the best and that what's made him great is the fact that he's always studied. He's always worked to develop his skills and physical (as well as mental) strength. He has put in time and effort to communicate his artistry the way that he's wanted to.

People often tell those who achieve something great that they are so lucky. "You're so lucky, you figured it all out," they say. And I think that we say the word *luck* because we miss what is really going on. We miss the fact that people get rewarded when they work hard. There is a cause and an effect to everything. Cause is the first action, the initiatory steps taken by the person to get stronger physically, emotionally, or mentally—the steps one takes to learn more.

Let's say you want to be an artist, you want to paint. You would need to start by painting more and reading about the stories of great painters. Or if you want to be a great musician, start practicing more. And if you want to be a great writer, start writing more.

Personally, I was born with almost no talent as a writer. I did extremely poorly in my English classes in school. I hardly passed. But when I got to college, I realized that writing was something I was interested in pursuing. I had no talent, so I developed my skill by looking at other writers. Some of my favorite writers at the time were F. Scott Fitzgerald and Hunter S. Thompson. I decided to research how Hunter S. Thompson learned to write. I discovered that he learned to write by retyping his favorite books over and over again. So I did the same thing. I taught myself to write by retyping my favorite books. I spent hours and hours developing my craft. I developed a strong work ethic and discipline because I had a glimpse of what I was capable of becoming and I wanted it to happen.

If you stink at something right now but would still love to pursue it as a hobby or as a career, do it anyway. You are not always going to be good at everything right away. Michael Jordan, arguably the greatest basketball player of all time, didn't make his varsity team as a sophomore. He wasn't skilled enough yet. He was particularly weak as a leader, so he became more humble, and spent hours and hours in the gym. Then, after his hard work, he was one of the top recruits out of high school and went to the University of North Carolina, one of the most prestigious basketball college programs in the world. He made it there not because of talent, but because he developed his skill.

At a certain point, talent is going to fail you. There are many talented athletes who don't make it. Perhaps this is because they don't take the time to develop their skills, and to take the responsibility of developing their work ethic. People who don't have work ethic can't get themselves out of a slump. This is because they aren't focused enough—they have raw, natural talent, but they don't take the time to develop it. Beethoven became a great composer and musician because he continuously practiced. Yes, he may have been talented when he began, but again, talent is only going to take you so far. And this is a truth that we see time and again throughout history.

Don't fool yourself into thinking that you're not good enough to do whatever it is that you want to do. Most people were not good enough when they started, but they had a deep affinity—a passion—for what they were doing, so they developed it into a skill. And later, they developed that skill into an obsession, that obsession into a profession, and so on. They became great by habit. By following this path, people become someone that they weren't before.

There's no substitute for hard work. There's no substitute for you and your efforts. You must be willing to arrive at the finish line of life with your body and your mind worn out, knowing that you have given it all you've got. There is no substitute for the peace that you will feel if you know that you have used your life to its fullest capacity, rather than relying on the talents that you were born with. To achieve great goals, or even to live a simple, joyful life, you must develop the skill of peace by doing the things you love more and more.

Success Doesn't Happen Overnight

I'm sure you've heard that Mozart was such a child prodigy that he produced quality orchestra music when he was only six years old. But there's one important detail missing from that story—when you go and look up the orchestras that play his music, they always play symphonies that he created in his early teen years, but never before. Why is that? Well, it's because the orchestra conductors chose not to perform his earlier symphonies because this work wasn't good enough.

Your skill level (or lack thereof) doesn't matter. What matters is that you keep taking consistent action. Success is hardly an overnight party—it's often years and years of work. Do not be discouraged if your results and skills are not where you want them to be right now. With consistent, continuous action you will arrive. Competency comes from unwavering consistency and dedication to your work. Do not let where you are get in the way of where you want to be. Every great artist, author, businessperson, and thinker was none of those things when they began. They became these things through their long-term, dedicated work.

We often overestimate what we can achieve in a year, and underestimate what we can achieve in a decade. For example, some people will have a goal like learning the guitar or starting a business, but after a month or two of starting they become so impatient with their progress, they give up and quit before they have even started. They want to be great right away, forgetting that becoming great happens with time.

It took basketball player LeBron James years to win his first NBA championship. It took rapper Eminem years of rapping, getting booed in small clubs in Detroit, before he was *discovered*. Dave

Matthews Band, one of the world's top-selling bands, spent three years selling CDs out of the trunk of a sedan and playing free gigs before stores started selling their albums and they started to make a living. And now they've sold half a billion dollars' worth of albums. It took Sylvester Stallone years as a broke scriptwriter before he sold *Rocky* and became a success. It was years of lost elections for Abe Lincoln before he became president. It was over a decade of playing without a Super Bowl championship that drove Ray Lewis, one of the greatest NFL linebackers ever, to lead his team to a championship in his final season as a professional.

What's the moral of these stories? Success, fulfillment, and purpose hardly ever happen overnight. Forget results—or lack thereof—and keep doing what you love. If you make what you love your obsession, you will become a master one day. And when you become a master, all of the failure you felt, the lack of money, and the stress will take care of itself— it will become a thing of the past. You will be fulfilled by your continual progress.

Proficiency Threshold

"It's really hard to get into the groove with things," a girl told me.

"Have you noticed we don't give things much time? We pick something new up, try it out, and since we don't excel immediately, we give up," I replied.

"But writing is a really hard thing to get in the groove with . . ." she said.

I told her, "So is everything." It's all the same. Generally, we quit before we even get semi-comfortable and develop our style. It takes time to be proficient and develop skills in anything. We must stick with it. This is our life, not some throwaway experience. So it's a threshold one must cross with anything: making music, shooting baskets, surfing, inventing products, and everything in between. Being proficient at anything takes time.

The best way to ensure that you never become great at anything is to try it out for a half hour, a few days, or a month, and then quit. This is why most New Year's resolutions fail. We don't stick to them.

We often don't realize that there's a *proficiency threshold* for all things. I'd argue that excellence isn't natural for any of us. You may have certain skills, but to make yourself great, you still have to cross the proficiency threshold. Everything takes time. The body, mind, and spirit must all align with your work before you get into a consistent groove. And this is only achieved by spending hours and hours working on your craft.

Some of the most impactful men and women of the twenty-first century are people who don't always see themselves as the most talented. They excel because of a deeply committed work ethic. They are comfortable with what they are doing because they have practiced so much that it becomes natural. They develop routines, rituals, and tools that enhance their productivity. They spend hours of committed time reaching the threshold of what they can handle.

Each person has a different threshold, and through self-exploration you will discover yours. You will have to spend hours and hours practicing, creating, studying, and doing. And one day you will begin to see your passion flowing through and out of you.

The Rule of Five

In the same way that the consistent watering of a seed planted in soil is essential for the seed to reach its destiny of becoming a plant, consistent work toward your vision is the only way you can see it manifest. Consistency is the only way you're going to live the life you want to live. Whether you want to live simply or lavishly is irrelevant. We need to be consistent because it's not what we do periodically that determines and shapes our lives, but what we do consistently. It's what we do each and every day that determines how we are living our lives. Jim Rohn, American entrepreneur, author, and motivational speaker, says, "Success is neither magical nor mysterious. Success is the natural consequence of consistently applying basic fundamentals." It's the ability to apply day in and day out what you know you have to do.

When Jack Canfield and Mark Victor Hansen released their first *Chicken Soup for the Soul* book, their goal was to sell a million and a half copies in a year and a half. Their publisher didn't believe it would be possible. So Canfield and Hansen began to study what they needed to do to make this dream come true.

During this time, they met a man who told them a story. He said, "Well, imagine that you are out in the forest and there's a humongous redwood tree that you would like to cut down. Do you think it would be best to stand out there swinging an axe as many times as you can for as long as you can? Or do you think it'd be better to use the axe to take five precise, strategic swings at the tree with all your strength each and every day till it comes down?" They replied, "Well, I think the second option is probably better." And the guy said, "Yes, if you take consistent action each and every day toward whatever it is that you want in life, eventually it's going to become a reality. It has to. As long as you stay consistent with it."

After hearing that story, Canfield and Hansen developed something called the Rule of Five. The Rule of Five is the commitment to do five things every single day that move you closer to your dreams. This is the formula that Canfield and Hansen developed to sell more than 500 million copies of the first *Chicken Soup for the Soul* book. Every day, they wrote down five different things that they had to do to move closer to their goal.

I encourage you to do the same. Make a list of the different things that you have to do. Ask yourself: how can I achieve this, feel this, help this person? And write down five different things that you can do. It could be contacting different people that you admire. It could be spending four hours studying. It could be going out and promoting yourself. It could be working on poetry, painting, or writing a chapter in a book each day. Or it could be building your website one day and stretching, doing yoga, or exercising the next day. It doesn't matter exactly what these things are, but they need to be five things that you feel move you closer to your goal. And the things can change each day, but there must be five.

The goal is that when you go to sleep at night, you know you've taken five positive steps toward your goal. And it doesn't matter how big your steps are—some days they might be smaller than others. What's important is that you're moving forward and getting closer to your goals—that life recognizes your consistent effort, energy, intention, and enthusiasm for them. When you do this, incredible things begin to happen. This is when people start to say, "Well, you're lucky." No, you're not lucky. You are putting in consistent action and life is starting to reward you for your efforts. New doors open in your life because you started to walk on the path to arrive at them.

When I launched my book *Into the Wind*, I applied the Rule of Five to help me reach my goals. Every day I did five things. One thing that really helped me was the Internet. In modern society in the Western world, we are blessed to have the Internet. If we focus long enough and work hard enough, we can make a living doing what we love with its help. I used this fact to my advantage, and within forty-eight hours my book was in the Top 300 books on all of Amazon. I went from being a completely unknown author that nobody had ever heard of and who had sold zero books, to changing thousands of people's lives, reaching my goals, and supporting myself—all because I used the Rule of Five. Every single day I contacted different people and asked them to share my book for me. I contacted my favorite authors and asked them to mentor me. I made YouTube videos and posted them on Facebook and Twitter. I contacted radio shows, and showed up for speaking events. I also gave copies of my book out for free sometimes. I did five things every single day, and now I'm here today literally living my dream.

The Rule of Five works. It worked for me and it can work for you. The trick is being consistent. It all depends on how disciplined you are. You need to be disciplined in the small things. What you eat, the books you read, all of the small things matter. These *small disciplines* need to be repeated with consistency every single day. They are what will lead to a higher quality of life. They lead to great achievements. You will get what you want by working slowly over time with consistency.

A lot of people do great things, but don't do them consistently. They have moments, whether it's a few hours a day, a few days a month, or a few weeks a year, where they feel sparks of greatness. But they have not yet learned how to ground their greatness. The way to do this, and develop greatness into a consistent characteristic, rather than a rare occurrence, is by consistently doing things that make you great, that make you confident, and that move you closer to your goal.

The more you do whatever it is you want to do, the more you

will develop. Your vision will change from something you didn't believe was possible to something you know is possible. If you stay consistent, you will feel it become a reality.

Practice the Rule of Five and bring it into your life for any and all of your goals. You can either make separate lists of five things you can do for each of your goals, and each of the ways you want to direct your energy, or you can make one Rule of Five list for your main vision and what's most important to you in your life. Both methods work in different circumstances. It all depends on you and what you want to do. But whatever you do, do it consistently.

The Ten-Minute Rule

If you want to be more consistent and get more things done, I have another exercise for you. It's called the Ten-Minute Rule. In Jack Canfield's book *The Success Principles*, he explains that he makes a list of the different things he wants to accomplish, a to-do list. Oftentimes many of us make to-do lists but don't actually do what is on them. To combat this problem, Jack separates everything that he can complete in ten to fifteen minutes or less, and then does those things immediately. Jack calls this the Ten-Minute Rule. By doing all the ten- or fifteen-minute tasks right away, you can finish up many things in one hour. And if you start your day doing those ten-minute things, you'll have an extremely productive day right from the start.

By implementing the Ten-Minute Rule into your life, and looking at the things you can do quickly in a short period of time, you will be much less stressed. Your list will seem less daunting because you'll be getting a lot of the little things done. And when you get the little things done, it makes a big difference.

Prioritizing

Prioritizing is a learned discipline. And you can't prioritize in a way that's true to what you really want until you learn about yourself through various experiences. You need to break away from your regular routine so you can prioritize your life in a way that coincides with what you want. Once you have experienced different ways of living, you will know what you need to prioritize.

By trying out different ways of living, I learned that I want to be an author who travels around and speaks about my writing. When I learned this, I realized what type of life I wanted to live. I wanted to create my own hours, write when I wanted to write, be my own boss, and have more time to reflect and think about life. By doing this, I heal myself and try to help other people, which is why I knew I needed to make this a priority and write more.

I wasn't a good writer as a kid, except in creative writing classes in school where we would make things up. Later, I realized that what I really didn't like about writing in school was sitting at a desk in class. So I had to prioritize making this easier for myself by practicing. I carried over the discipline I learned from basketball, and taught myself how to write by retyping *The Great Gatsby* over and over again. I remember spending summer break between freshman and sophomore years sitting at my desk and retyping the book every day. From sports, I learned to look at who was doing the best, find out how they were doing so well, and copy their work ethic and secrets. So I decided to do the same for writing. When I found out that one of my favorite authors, Hunter S. Thompson, had dropped out of middle school and learned to write by retyping *The Great Gatsby*, it was enough to inspire me to do the same. By my third and final semester in college, I did little to no required schoolwork.

Instead, I wrote and read all day and night. And by the time I got back from traveling, after I dropped out, I had to rearrange my life to write my book.

Seeing what we need to do to rearrange our lives is easy, but actually doing it is hard. But why is it so hard? Why wouldn't we want to do what we know will bring us the most satisfaction in life? No one has created a five-step process explaining how to get yourself to do the things you know you need to do so your life will be as good as you want it to be. That's because it's common sense. Just do it, even if you don't want to. In the end, it's what will bring you the most satisfaction.

Chapter 10

Accumulation and Application of Knowledge

The only thing that interferes with my learning is my education.

—ATTR. ALBERT EINSTEIN

A man once told me, "A person who knows a little about many things is of no use to me, except perhaps in a long car ride because they would be able to briefly entertain me on many subjects. But if I need a task done, give me an expert." At the time I didn't quite understand what he was saying. However, now I realize what he meant. Most of us never really commit to mastering anything—or at least becoming really great at something. Instead, we often fill our heads with a lot of senseless things—like what the billboards or the Kardashians say. I now understand that this man was referring to the separation between general and specific knowledge.

We all know that information is of great value. Sometimes a piece of information is the difference between making a living doing what you love or having to compromise on the life you've imagined. And sometimes information can be a matter of life and death. Yes, information is extremely valuable.

In school we're taught loads of information. If we wish to be *educated*, we must memorize most of it as efficiently as possible. The more mistakes we make and the harder time we have memorizing it, the lower our level of intelligence is in the eyes of institutionalized education. But that kind of intelligence can only get us so far. There are highly educated people who never do anything with their lives. And there are *uneducated* people who empower the world.

In *Think and Grow Rich*, Napoleon Hill states that there are two types of knowledge—general knowledge and specific knowledge. General knowledge includes information such as historical facts and simple how-to instructions, information like the year Columbus sailed the ocean blue. Specific knowledge, on the other hand, is knowledge that is important for your dreams, lifestyle, beliefs, and career. Specific knowledge is knowing the fact that you first must create a book proposal in order to publish a book. You need to know this if you're an author, or wish to become one.

It seems pretty clear that for us to become more valuable in our line of work, or in our relationships, we need to learn more of the specific knowledge that's important to us. If you wanted to try to make more money, you'd need to know that most independently wealthy people have written down their financial goals. General knowledge can be entertaining and important, but it's not significant or useful for acquiring what is important to us. A lot of what we memorize for entertainment purposes, or to do well on tests, ends up being useless. The value of specific knowledge, on the other hand, increases with time because you use it to reach a goal or an objective that's of importance to you.

Give me the name of anyone who was *great* in the eyes of the world, and I can assure you that they know little about most other things. This is true because they put all their focus into learning and practicing one thing. I doubt that Mozart could tell you about how to instill democracy, or knew the laws of thermodynamics. I am sure Steve Jobs didn't know how to build the engine of a car, or all the types of pale ale beers. That's because these people filled their brains with specific knowledge about their area of interest— they didn't waste time learning about things that weren't useful for their work. So learn more about your area of interest. Read anecdotes about successful people, quotes from them, strategies, and other information specific to your work.

Although he loved baseball, Michael Jordan did not become a Hall of Fame basketball player by spending an equal amount of time learning golf, baseball, and basketball. He dedicated most of his life to the one thing he loved the most—basketball.

Time and again, I hear the greatest achievers and influencers of the twenty-first century saying, "It's about the only thing I am good at," when they talk about their area of expertise. And I believe there's something to that. They all found something they enjoyed doing, became good at it, made it their obsession, then their profession, and they've never really had to work a day in their lives. What they did not do is find ten things that were fun, try a different one every week, and never commit to just one thing. They picked one thing and let it become an all-consuming obsession.

This became clear when I interviewed Bucky Lasek. "I'm just obsessive. I have a single focus to be the best, and to get better every day," he said. And he really does work every day. Lasek created a large skate bowl in his own backyard, and practices five hours a day. What I really noticed about Lasek is that he doesn't put his energy into *too* many things, only skating and his family. "All my focus for years was just on how I could learn the next trick, and improve myself as a skater."

I believe we would surprise ourselves if we committed but a year of our lives to becoming an expert at something. This is one of the keys to success for many of the world's peak performers. To make even a modest living doing what you love is not necessarily easy. It's not possible unless you commit to it full time. Not sometimes, not just when the time feels right, not only when you are free. It can't be a closet hobby, or something you do when you're in the mood. It takes real focus to become the best you can be. Sometimes this may even mean burning other bridges—the other plans and escape routes in life if it all falls apart—you know, the plan B and plan C. You need to see no other way out except living the life you've imagined.

One of my favorite musicians is Bob Dylan, and I spend a lot of time learning about the people I truly admire. One thing that I found interesting about Dylan is that, compared to many musicians, his sound was average. One time I heard a quote about him that said, "The guy wasn't born great. He just carried a guitar everywhere he went. The guy was always strumming." And I think there's an important lesson there. The more specific your focus, the greater your results.

We all know of the tale of the educated person. He was so educated that he had two undergraduate degrees from an Ivy League school and a master's degree. He had achieved just about all one could in the world of formal education. But then he spent the rest of his life paying off student loan debt, working for other people in jobs he was overqualified for, and was always underpaid.

Then there is the story of the other person across town. He barely graduated from high school and dropped out of college because he didn't think it taught him anything other than tasteless information about generalized subjects. Then, he decided he wanted to be a businessperson, so he began studying business strategies and self-help principles obsessively, and twenty years later he became a billionaire.

Do not waste all your years with information that has no value to your vision. Leave it for someone else who may find passion in it. Focus on what you do best.

Education

One of the greatest tragedies of human existence is when we stop learning. The word *education* comes from the Latin root word *educo*, which means "to educe," or draw from within. That's what education really means. We can never cease to do that because then our spirit will die. You will cease to feel the beauty, surprises, and pain of life. When we continue to learn new things, we can better our lives and ourselves, and share our gifts with the world. Many people quit learning, start watching five hours of TV a day, and lie and say that they only watch about an hour of it. That's America. Business philosopher Jim Rohn once said, "Walk away from the ninety-five percent. Don't do what they do. Don't eat what they eat. Don't follow the way that they are following."

The majority of us immediately close ourselves off to learning new things in life. Traditional education lasts until somewhere in our mid-twenties if we go through higher education. But is it really *higher?*

Couldn't the highest form of education be the discipline of getting to know one's self? Isn't this the greatest form of knowledge? What could be greater than understanding who you are and what you love? What's more important than knowing what your talents and skills are? And shouldn't you have a clear understanding about what's important to you and how you feel? Being comfortable with who you are is the greatest form of education that exists and, unfortunately, most of us never test out this type of education because there's no degree for it. And most of us want degrees and certificates—we want other people to tell us what's important to learn and what isn't important to learn.

Being truly educated means that you must be mature. You must realize that it's your responsibility to find out what you need to learn. It doesn't matter whether it's how to start a business, becoming aware of how you react to situations, or noticing your habits—you need to take the responsibility to learn about it. And when you do, when I do, when other people do, all of us together will have a truly educated society—an education that won't cease to exist when we get out of class, because it will stay with us until we die.

But until that happens, it doesn't matter how old you are. There are always things for you to learn, and things for you to share to inspire others. However, this is only possible if we continue to learn, to try new things, to notice what feels good, to notice what doesn't feel good, and to be aware of what we want to know more about.

Knowing the way of ourselves is how we return home, even while we continue to move through the world to different places and experiences. We remain centered when we are connected with ourselves. This is what it means to draw from within. This is what it means to be educated.

The Desire to Be Educated

Someone asked me, "Do you even have a degree?" They asked it as if my work is irrelevant without one. I couldn't help but laugh. I knew that this person (though they put a lot of emphasis on their own degrees) had no idea what the true definition of education was. So I asked this person, "Why does anyone need a piece of paper to let others know they are credible if they can produce results instead?" He couldn't answer the question.

Results are the mark of an educated person, not how many papers they have with stamps on them. There are all too many scholars and people of education who achieve absolutely nothing in their lives. Sure, there are many uneducated people who don't either, but those who've left their mark on the universe have primarily been uneducated. They have been the ones who've altered human history. In fact, the top people in nearly every industry never graduated college: Richard Branson (business), Steve Jobs (technology), Brad Pitt (entertainment), Ellen DeGeneres (media/entertainment), Mark Zuckerberg (technology), James Cameron (entertainment), Henry Ford (business), Thomas Edison (inventor), Pablo Picasso (artist), Walt Disney (entertainment), Bill Gates (technology), David Karp (technology), and on and on and on and on and on. All the people on this list had the ability to see infinite possibilities and make them their life's work. They made what they wanted to see happen into reality, not content to let their dreams remain just a figment of their imaginations.

The definition of an educated person should be someone who has the ability to organize their desires and use knowledge, planning, and strategy to obtain them—to literally go out there and acquire it. Isn't that the point of education in the first place? Shouldn't it help groom us to make results in the real world? And why the heck would anyone go to school if they knew they could create the results they desired without it?

Famous author Napoleon Hill once said, "An educated person is one who has so developed the faculties of his mind that he may acquire anything he wants, or its equivalent, without violating the rights of others." So why should I (or anyone, for that matter) clutter up my mind with general knowledge, memorizing stuff that other people say is important, for the purpose of answering questions I don't want to answer so I can be thought of as an *educated person*? Especially when there's a wealth of power, knowledge, and potential within each of us that can supply us with anything we require?

Intentionally Naive vs. Ignorantly Naive

We know too much. We know all the formulas and definitions and historical dates and rules and book information—we're often so stuck in our heads that we block ourselves from experimenting with our life experience, and from learning on the go.

It's said that there was a dialogue between Beethoven and one of his students that went like this:

STUDENT: "How do I write symphonies?"
MOZART: "Begin with minuets."
STUDENT: "But you were writing symphonies when you were only nine!"
MOZART: "Well, I never asked anyone how to do it."

Mozart is explaining that it's better to be innocently unprepared and passionately overambitious than it is to be exceptionally prepared by overthinking. The problem with people is that we know all the facts, formulas, procedures, and history, yet we do not know how to listen to our inner guidance.

Our mind is overcrowded with external information, which leaves no room for us to listen to the inner voice. In Steve Jobs's

Stanford commencement speech, he said, "Stay hungry, stay foolish." It means be overly ambitious and forget all the reasons why your dreams are "impossible." Be like a little kid chasing their dreams. Trust that your passion can guide you, even if you feel like you're not prepared enough to begin taking action.

Give me a person who knows nothing other than the fact that they can achieve anything with time, and they will do just that—if they keep working every day.

Habits

> The chains of habit are too weak to be felt until they are too strong to be broken.
>
> —Samuel Johnson

My life doesn't go as well when I'm unaware of my habits. T. Harv Eker, author, businessman, and motivational speaker, says there are two types of habits—habits of doing and habits of not doing. We realize the habits of doing a lot—the things we're putting into motion constantly. But we often don't see the habits of not doing. I used to always get in the habit of not getting uncomfortable, not getting out of my routine, not seeing the positive, not writing my goals down, not following my passions, and not having faith in something larger than myself. When I realized this, I started to develop new habits, like consistently trying to get myself in uncomfortable situations where I feel overwhelmed, and situations where I feel the task is too big to complete. I like to do this now because I learn much more about myself.

Bob Marley said, "You never know how strong you are until being strong is the only choice that you have." I think it's important to put ourselves in situations that build the habit of taking action, situations where the only choice is to be strong and positive. The more we put ourselves in those situations, the more our life continues to improve, and the more we continue to grow. We need to look at our habits of not doing—like not following our dreams, or not setting our goals, or not eating well—because we need to be honest with ourselves to make changes.

Be aware of what you are not doing as well. Perhaps you aren't good at selling, choosing a direction, being kind to others, or smiling, and start to work on making changes in these areas. Or work with people who can help you do things you aren't good at. You need to know the truth to better your life. Where you go is a result of what you do, both consciously and unconsciously. Be especially aware of your habits—what you do or don't do over sustained periods of time.

"Routine" Exercise

Look at your morning routine. Is it stressing you out or getting you prepared for a confident day? Be honest with yourself in all areas of your life. You know which habits are killing you and which are enhancing your life. Take inventory of all your habits. Need to drink more water? Need to write things down? Need to stop being so passive? Need to exercise more? Need to study more? Need to meditate or do yoga? Need to eat better? Think about what you can do to improve your life and do it!

Chapter 11

Thoughts Become Things

Positive thinking will let you do everything better than negative thinking will.

—ZIG ZIGLAR, AMERICAN AUTHOR, SALESMAN,
AND MOTIVATIONAL SPEAKER

To be happy and fulfilled you must stay positive despite the fact that everything around you seems negative to the physical senses. And the only way we can do this is by remembering that there's a time lapse between defining and discovering what we want and then taking action to make it happen. There's a time lapse between starting to do what we want, and its manifestation in reality. That time lapse always varies in duration. It's a complete mystery.

You must remember this to keep your mind focused and your heart centered on your vision. Understanding this fundamental law of life can help you get what you want, live how you want to live, and help who you want to help. You can do it as long as you trust that it will happen in due time. Just stay focused on the thing you want to do.

Esther Hicks, American inspirational speaker and bestselling author, explains that it's really important to be aware of what you are focusing on. You are either focusing on what you want or focusing on what you don't want. This is really important to know because it makes or breaks your opportunity to make your dreams manifest. For example, if you want to make money, and only focus on the fact that you don't have money, you're focusing your physical senses on the reality that is—and this is a mistake. It is not effective to put more energy into the reality that you don't have money, friendship, romance, the right career, or certain characteristics. Focusing on these negative outcomes and things you don't want simply beckons your mind to keep re-creating similar circumstances.

It's super-important to stay positive. Your mind creates what you focus on the most. Stay focused on what you want to dream into reality. Use your imagination to connect to the new way of living, which is different from the reality that you have previously been experiencing with your physical senses. Remember, if you wish to be a visionary—a highly fulfilled, purpose-driven, and effective human being—you must create from your imagination. Be creative, find your gifts, and share them with the world.

Watch Your Words

In the book *Words Can Change Your Brain* by Andrew Newberg and Mark Waldman, we learn that neuroscience has proven that certain words you think or say create how you feel. When planes are in flight, the word *attitude* refers to the angle of the flight path in relation to the horizon. When the nose of the plane is raised or lowered, the attitude changes. In life, the way you think about a problem you're facing creates your attitude.

The book suggests eliminating the word *problem* from your

vocabulary, because it invokes stress and fear. Instead, the book suggests using words like *challenge* or *situation*. If you think of something as a challenge, rather than a problem, it's a chance to rise to the occasion—it's much less debilitating, and creates less chaos and tenseness in the mind and body. Being conscious of your word choices can help you focus on the positive, rather than what is bad, wrong, and problematic. American industrialist Henry Kaiser once said, "Problems are only opportunities in work clothes." Problems are simply challenges where we must rise to the occasion, get to work, and find the solution.

The words we say have a great influence on our emotions and lives. Author Henry Tuckerman explained this truth best when he said, "It is amusing to detect character in the vocabulary of each person. The adjectives habitually used, like the inscriptions of a thermometer, indicate the temperament." So we must try to be aware of our language—because what we say and think often becomes a part of who we are.

When feeling doubtful, or in conflict, I often erroneously use the word *if*. *If* I can complete this task . . . and many of us use *if* when we describe our goals, dreams, and desires.

One of the most influential philosophers of the twentieth century, J. Krishnamurti, said, "Do it or don't do it, but just get on with it." All too often we forget that if we really want something, and don't give up, we can achieve it. But instead, most of us think that our destiny is left up to chance and we doubt that our dreams are possible. We say *if*. A highly effective person never uses the word *if*. Instead they use *as* or *when*.

Take a look at the following statements:

1. When this or something better happens . . .
2. If this happens . . .

Do you agree that statement 1 is more positive?

Highly functioning individuals know that using the words *this or something better* opens them up to positive results, while using the word *if* means that you don't understand the magnitude of your potential to create the life you want. When saying *when* or *as* instead of *if*, you imply that it's going to happen, that you won't give up until it does or until something even better happens. You are providing the space for good things to happen.

We often say *if* because we are scared of the pressure that saying *when* entails. If we say *if*, we're kind of saying that it's okay if what we want to have happen doesn't happen. This is a negative type of psychology because it doesn't create the sense of urgency that is present when we say that something *will* happen. For many of us, saying that something *will* happen is stressful, because it puts pressure on us. That is why, especially when speaking to yourself (to first build the habit), and eventually when speaking to others, it's important to say, "When this happens or something better. . . ." When you do this, you are saying that you deserve what you want, and should get it in due time, or something better will happen. There is no need to settle for anything less than your highest potential. So start by eliminating the doubt-implying word *if* from your vocabulary when talking about your dreams!

Scientists can prove that everything in the world is energy. When we look under an electron microscope, we see that what appears to be solid is actually energy in vibration that creates different forms, shapes, and levels of solidity (from wood to gas). This fundamental law of nature is inclusive to humans as well. We are energy. If your heart or brain stops producing and transmitting energy, you die. When you're in the hospital, the electrocardiograph (EKG) measures the electrical impulse of your heart. And when that machine stops, or *flatlines*, you're dead.

The late Steve Jobs once said that innovation is merely connecting the dots. And that is what I'm asking you to do with me here—connect the dots. Everything is energy, including our emotions. Scientists can now measure thoughts, and their electrical impulses. Okay, so that means that how good we feel and how well our lives are going is contingent upon our energy levels. So it's important to increase our energy. How do we do that? With the thoughts and words that we choose to give life to, whether they are negative or positive. For example, have you ever noticed that as soon as you say, "I can't do that," "It's impossible," or "I'm not ready," then it feels as though you really can't do it? That's because you're using words that tell your subconscious mind that there's no use in trying.

When I interviewed Laird Hamilton, he told me a story about a woman who approached him on the beach. She knew that he was one of the greatest surfers alive and so she asked him to help her: "Excuse me, can you please teach me how to surf, because I really suck?" Hamilton told her to say, "I am good at surfing" and to stop saying that she sucked. The woman said it and Hamilton told her that this was her first surf lesson.

Creating the results we want is mostly psychological. It starts in our minds, and then becomes our thoughts and words, which describe what type of world we believe we live in, which eventually turns into the world we see and experience. Albert Einstein said that the most important decision to make is whether you live in a friendly or hostile world. In the twenty-first century, the biggest choice we make is whether our life is full of possibilities or impossibilities. Impossibilities are expressed with phrases like, "This is too hard," "I can't do it," and "It's impossible." And when we give these phrases life with the energy of our attention, we paralyze ourselves from taking actions—if we believe something has no hope, what's the use anyway? And even if we don't paralyze ourselves, and we do take action, our vocabulary of impossibilities has still conditioned us to think in terms of limitations.

When I was little, I remember my brother and I used to always play a game where whoever saw a punch-buggy (a Volkswagen Beetle) and said "punch-buggy" would get to punch the other person until the loser saw another one. I had a sore arm while in the car with my older brother because I also always seemed to lose. I used to say, "You always see the punch-buggies!" And he did. Now I realize it may, in fact, have been because I kept reinforcing that belief by complaining that he always saw them! While this is a small-scale example, perhaps you can see where it relates to your own life—look for the things you unconsciously say or tell yourself that just *keep* happening.

"No one makes money as an artist" is one I hear all the time. First of all, it's not true. Some people make a lot of money as artists. And secondly, when we say things like that, we program our minds to create a reality that proves our beliefs to us, one where no one makes any money as an artist. Our minds look for evidence to prove that what we're thinking is right. Before we even begin to take action, we've often convinced ourselves about what's possible and impossible, simply by the words we use.

Focus on replacing negative words with more positive ones such as, "I can do this," or "I know it's possible to . . ." Just say these out loud—see how much more empowering those words are? You will feel your whole body and voice change.

Another big place we hang ourselves up is when we say, "I am not (fill in the blank) enough." Some common ones are: not smart enough, pretty enough, old enough, young enough, talented enough, skinny enough, experienced enough, and so on. Again, if you tell yourself you're not good or deserving enough, then what type of situation is your mind going to create? One that proves your vocabulary—that you are not (fill in the blank) enough.

Because we fear failure, we forget that some of the smartest yet least educated people have succeeded with their goals. As have the most overweight, the skinniest, the oldest, and the youngest. Our chance for success is more related to how we see the world than to how the world actually is. Life responds to our thoughts—if you believe you're not ready or experienced enough, that's what you'll experience.

Think Your Purpose

You are today where your thoughts have brought you; you will be tomorrow where your thoughts take you.

—James Allen

Life becomes more meaningful when we see the power that we each possess as individuals. One of our greatest powers is the power of our thoughts. One of our greatest times of powerlessness is when we don't see the value and worth of our own thoughts and mind. We often recognize the greatness and potential of other people's minds, even though their thoughts are probably quite similar to our own. The difference is that we don't stay focused on those thoughts and act accordingly. Your thoughts have the ability to change, transform, and better any part of your life, any part of society, and any part of someone else's life. You must consistently direct your thoughts to where you want them to be, to where you really, really want to go in your life. The more you start consciously directing your thoughts, the more this new habit will take hold and help you in your life.

My e-mail signature reads, "Miracles are normal." A "miracle" is something that logical or rational thinking can't explain. I meet the most incredible people in the most unusual circumstances. Some people may call these events *coincidences*, but I know that they are miracles. I made that phrase my e-mail signature because in the millisecond that I or someone else reads it, the energy is being sent out into the universe to make something incredible—something blow-our-minds-it's-so-good—happen.

I used to always think that something bad was waiting around the corner. "I can't seem to get a break!" I used to say. Freshman year in college I realized that I was living that way and I got honest with myself. I learned by studying and through experience that my thoughts were actually influencing and creating a lot of my life and all of my feelings. I realized how negative my thoughts had been.

Our thoughts become habitual patterns, and then they become a repeating cycle that turns into our way of seeing the world. We choose a cycle of thoughts to think in—whether they are self-defeating, or enhancing, absolutely incredible, beautiful, peaceful, and fulfilling. No matter the way you think, you need to take responsibility and be aware so you can create the feelings that you want to feel. Remember, you can think any way you want.

When I learned about the power of my thoughts, I began to journal. I would say different thinking-enhancing affirmations over and over again. I spent about thirty minutes a day just writing down that I was living a better, more peaceful life—that I was successful doing what I love, that I was proud of myself, that I forgave myself, that my life was getting better and better, that I was receiving more exciting news, and that I was meeting interesting, successful, good-hearted people. I told myself these things for a long time consistently, and four years later I'm living my dream.

Part of my dream was writing books and poetry, giving speeches, and sharing what I had learned in other creative ways. This is what brings me the most joy, and I realized that I could live in my highest joy if I could use my thoughts to my advantage. And so can you!

When you consistently and constantly improve your thoughts and reflect on the way you've been thinking, you can live any way you want. So think big! Think courageously. Think positively. Think creatively. Think responsibly. Think differently. Think out of love. And think out of confidence.

Value Your Thoughts

Remember, happiness doesn't depend upon who you are or what you have. It depends solely upon what you think.

—Dale Carnegie, American writer and lecturer

In an interview, I heard Jay-Z explain that when you see someone who has achieved a high level of success, something that's noteworthy, you've got to ask, *how?* How did they get there? How did they do that? So now, when someone catches my attention for the quality of work that they do, I ask, *how?*

Actor Will Smith is someone I admire for the depth of commitment he has to his work. So I asked myself *how?* How did Will Smith get there? Through the beautiful conveniences of the Internet (which you should take advantage of, too) you can discover so much information. There's a YouTube video of Will talking about his different beliefs, and his truth. He says that thoughts are things—that thoughts have a physical impact on life. He believes that if you dream something, and picture it clearly, you've just made that real—and from there, you do what you've got to do. He believes that if you say you can't do something, you make that fact real. Your thoughts create your feelings and beliefs, and whatever you believe about the world you create.

But Will Smith isn't the only person who's created awesome things and inspired a lot of people in the world. I think that—at least eight out of ten times—happy, fulfilled, successful, creative, healthy, wealthy people live this way because they understand the power that their thoughts have.

Everything is energy, and if you match and sustain (as Albert Einstein once said) the frequency of that which you desire, then you can't help but get it. Pointing your thoughts in the direction of what you want and how you want to feel should be your main focus. You can't control every situation in life, but you can control the way that you respond to them. If something seems negative, you can still focus on the positive things and on what you can take out of the situation to empower yourself. The one thing that you can create is how you feel. Other things can have influence on how you feel, but ultimately, what something means to you is your choice, and it all begins with your thoughts.

The more you value your thoughts, the more you realize the power that you have, and the potential that you are. And the more that you realize all of this, the more you will innately see your self-worth and value. You will realize how much you matter, and that you're capable and important. You'll realize that life can be as beautiful as you let it be. Life will begin to take on a whole new meaning.

Ask the Right Questions

When you ask the right questions, you get the right answers. And sometimes you find answers where you least expect them. But once you've received the answer, you'll know. Receiving the answers to your prayers, dreams, and questions is an amazing experience. However, to get there you must first ask the right questions more often. Ask, and you will receive. Consciously direct questions in the right way, just as you do with your thoughts, and life will gift you the answers to your questions.

A question that I've often asked throughout this book is, *How?* How did certain people turn out the way they did? How do they do what they do? How do they feel what they feel, and how do they live how they live? Another *how* is *how can I . . . ?* How can I experience this? How can I have this? How can we do this together? How will this be possible?

We can also ask these types of questions in our visualizations. *How can something become a reality? Where am I going?* Ask, and then see and feel everything connected and working together in an incredible fashion, full of exciting events.

When we mess up in life or when things go wrong, we often have thoughts like, *Why am I stupid? Why is this messed up? Why am I so prone to failure? Why is my life always getting worse?* And when you ask these questions, your mind looks for the answers. It says, *Because you're stupid, you aren't pretty enough, you don't look good enough, you don't have straight enough teeth*, but all of those things are part of the beautiful mess that make up who we are.

When we can accept this truth, we can ask more enhancing questions: How can I improve upon this? How can I improve upon my feelings? How can I better my life and myself? How can I better my life and the lives of those in my community? How can I feel more alive? How? How? How?

When you ask these questions, you're bringing them to the attention of your subconscious mind. Your subconscious mind often works in images. When you ask a question, your subconscious mind produces images within milliseconds. It happens before you can even cognize them within your imagination.

Chapter 12

Innovation over Duplication

Innovation distinguishes a leader from a follower.

—STEVE JOBS

We hear a lot about the success of Steve Jobs and his creations. Some talk about his manic work ethic, his diet, his spirituality, and how he loved what he did, while others say that he achieved success because he was a total jerk. I have a different take from all of the above. I believe that the true reason for Jobs's success is extremely practical yet overlooked.

Jobs never asked prospective customers what they wanted. He didn't check the marketplace for competition, nor did he study buyer trends. He didn't care what people wanted. He believed what they really wanted was something they felt was *the best*. Jobs said, "You can't just ask customers what they want and then try and give that to them. By the time you get it built, they'll want something new," and "Our goal is to make the best devices in the world, not to be the biggest," and "We made the buttons on the screen look so good you'll want to lick them."

His focus was not on giving people what they thought they wanted, but on creating something that didn't yet exist. On making something so good that people would naturally gravitate toward it. That's innovation. Innovation is creating a demand for something because of the intention and attention that can be felt in its essence. Jobs said, "Be a yardstick of quality."

One could argue that the sole motive behind most businesses of all industries is profit. Profit is the bottom line. But Jobs didn't see it this way. For Jobs, excellence was the bottom line. Excellence would then create profit and change the world. And because this excellence was etched into all his work, he made history.

The fact is that Jobs's bottom line of excellence couldn't be more distinguishable than when he left Apple. When he was first forced out, the company started to go downhill. He felt they were compromising quality for profit. If your goal is to create something that will withstand the test of time, it's important that you do not cut corners or compromise your product to generate more profit. When Apple realized they were headed toward their doom, they got Jobs to come back to fix everything. He brought excellence, intention, and innovation back—and Apple launched to even higher heights of success than they'd ever been before. And look at them now!

Jobs changed human history because he didn't settle until he found what he loved to do. He demanded excellence from himself and those around him. He worked with discipline and didn't cut corners. He valued quality over quantity of revenue, because when you do, revenue will come. That's what made Jobs an innovator. He looked within himself, came up with ideas, and created them because he was passionate. He created them with obsessive focus on excellence and believed that that would generate customers naturally.

Yet, in today's world, most of us are replicators. We replicate everything from our ideas to what we wear. Replicators can be successful, but they will never be innovative, because they just look to see what's selling and trendy, and cash in on the trends. In the market today, too many people slump on the creative aspect of products for the sake of profit. There are too few visionaries because most give up vision to obey popular opinions.

Jobs described the standard of excellence and how to do great things when he said, "When you're a carpenter making a beautiful chest of drawers, you're not going to use a piece of plywood on the back, even though it faces the wall and nobody will ever see it. You'll know it's there, so you're going to use a beautiful piece of wood on the back." Jobs never compromised on quality. He wouldn't have ever used plywood, even if he could have had a bigger return.

Business, people, and the world are all in need of quality and excellence over quantity. This begins by trusting your own vision, not by following the marketplace. Be a visionary. Be an innovator. Don't be a follower. Create what's within you.

Bob Dylan

We are fighting now to save that endangered species—the individual.

—Marty Rubin

Bob Dylan is arguably one of the greatest songwriters who has ever lived, and is certainly one of the most well-known and successful musicians of the twenty-first century. Dylan has created hundreds of albums and has never stopped. Even, as of this writing, at seventy-three years old, he continues to tour. Dylan stands out because of his persistence and willingness to be different.

The thing that's made Dylan so special is that although people have always classified him as a folk musician, he stretched out of the folk music box. He achieved his success because he wrote lyrics that were different from other folk musicians'. He was outspoken and didn't conform to the traditions of folk music. He wrote political, activist songs that questioned authority. At the time, this was unheard of and many other folk musicians denounced him. Dylan didn't let this affect him because he wasn't living his passion to be accepted—he was living it to express himself and let it flow through him. He wanted to share what he wanted to share, and create what he wanted to create—and continues to do so to this day.

If there's anything that you can learn from this extremely successful artist, it's that you must be consistent with your creativity. If you're a creative person, if you are an artist, don't stop! Don't ever stop creating. Don't get lost trying to figure out all these other things that you have to do to be successful. Work on them, but stay focused on what you do best, whatever that is. What Bob did best was write beautiful lyrics and new melodies, so he focused on that and kept doing it every day. Second, he didn't try to fit into any molds. No matter what your particular passion is, don't try to fit the mold and what's trending. Just do you. Do what's best for you and don't conform. Don't conform to a particular part of the marketplace, to a particular way that business is done or art is done, or to a particular form of relationships.

Do things the way that you feel is best. Follow your heart and don't try to be accepted by other people, because you'll never receive approval from everyone. It's a never-ending cycle that will always leave you discontent. You can't please everyone, no matter how hard you try. Focus on what you do best, be consistent with it, and everything will fall into place.

Also, you must never give up. Dylan's success didn't come overnight; it came because he decided that he would never give up. He was even homeless at times and slept on people's couches. He played anywhere and everywhere that he could to consistently build momentum, confidence, and experience.

You must do the same. Build momentum, confidence, and experience. Keep being consistent, and be different. Everything will open up.

Nonconformity

Don't get stuck doing what the world, your parents, and your friends ask you to do. If that becomes a habit, it restricts your freedom. Oftentimes you don't even realize that it's restricting your freedom because it's all you know. You start to descend into a downward spiral and your new physiology becomes a mediocre, average level of your potential, rather than one that recognizes the greatness and uniqueness that you are. *Not conforming* to what the world asks of you is the birthplace of your greatness.

Don't yield to popular opinions, trends, and fads. None of them are real, and none of them are you. They're for other people, and you are not other people. You are *you*. You are your own person. Don't dress the way the media says you should dress, and don't listen to music just because it's on the radio. Find out what *you* like.

All of the greatest achievers, social contributors, and people who are considered the voices of their generation were all nonconformists. They created their world the way they wanted it to be created, not the way it was already created. They followed their own path, rather than being led by the mind, which is conditioned by our world to think and behave in certain ways.

We all want freedom. I never met someone who said they wanted to be enslaved. But freedom is only possible when we first live with independence. And independence is nonconformity. You can never be fulfilled unless you are being independent—without independence you're not being yourself.

Whether you want a higher quality of life or to achieve a big goal makes no difference. Regardless, you need to do something differently than how it's been done for the last hundreds of thousands of years. You need to look at the world your own way. Stop looking through the lenses that society tries to put on your eyes. You have to respectfully decline the views, beliefs, opinions, and fears of the world around you. You have to detach from the chains of conclusions that you have not come to on your own.

To be a nonconformist means forming your own conclusions about who you are. You need to figure out what's possible and what life is about. Look at institutions, religions, work, careers, your physical body, relationships, spirituality, how you spend your time, money, rules, laws, and schools from your own unique perspective. You have to form your own opinions about all of these things. Otherwise, your mind is being controlled by social consensus.

If you look deeper, with a discerning eye, you'll realize that following trends won't set you free—you'll be just another number. You'll be put into a box and placed in a neat row next to everyone else. You need to climb out of the box, and when you do, other people will see you, and they will climb out too.

Nonconformity creates a domino effect. When other people see it, they are inspired and they want to do it too. Nonconformity isn't chaos, like many people would like you to think. Nonconformity is order. It's order created by experience. Staying in the box doesn't allow you to experience that which you must experience. You simply experience what everyone else wants you to get out of life.

Ralph Waldo Emerson once said, "Whoso would be a man, must be a nonconformist." He said that quite some time ago, so I would like to modernize that statement by saying, "Whoso would be a true living person, must be a nonconformist." If you want to be fully alive, and know yourself on a deeper level, you can only do this by not conforming and by finding out what you are, what your tastes are, how strong you are, and how capable you are. When we begin to do this together, all the systems of control, oppression, and lies will fall away and become obsolete. We will no longer be dependent—we will be interdependent.

When you live from your truth, and your truth is different from that of other people, you can help them and they can help you. You will both open up and see different points of view, which will further help both of you understand your truth. This is so much healthier than being dependent on government and Hollywood to educate and entertain us. So many organized institutions are nothing more than illusions that simply perpetuate popular opinion.

The birthplace of all creativity is nonconformity. The birthplace of appreciating life comes from nonconformity. The only people who have ever changed the world have been nonconformists. You must not conform to belief systems that don't enliven you.

The Wright brothers were nonconformists to the belief that you couldn't take a piece of metal, bend it, and fly it. They didn't conform to the standardized belief of the industry. When they created and flew that plane, they seemingly defied the beliefs of those around them.

Don't feel afraid of what others will think of you. If someone thinks of you in a negative way, it's simply because they are threatened by you. They are threatened by your stepping out of the box because it forces them to look and reflect on their own life. So don't take heed of their words. If you don't like the way something is, don't conform to it.

You must live your life the way you want your life to be lived. If you don't, then you are hardly living at all. If you go through life casually and ordinarily, you will become a casualty. *Oh, it was so sad that Billy was never able to live life the way he wanted to. He was such a nice person. He always did what everybody asked of him. He will always be remembered as someone who caused little trouble.* But do you really want to cause no trouble at all? Cause a bit of trouble. Experience a bit of disorder, a bit of chaos. Get to know what real order is so that you can live according to your own constitution, and your own principles. (But I will repeat again that this doesn't give you a license to maliciously harm anyone or steal.)

When you know what your principles are, stand for them. Do not conform to the principles of others if they are not your principles. Do not be subservient to someone or something that wants to bow down and control you. The only thing that you need to answer to is the higher order of life, the higher intelligence of life—your own soul and love. You don't have to answer to anything else. Don't conform to things or people who have put on a mask and cried out that you must follow them. Only you know what you love, and only you know what your soul is asking you to do. Don't follow the herd or you will step in other people's shit.

Independence

Do you want to be independent of other people's opinions of you, or trapped within the confines of doubt from their words? Before you answer the question, consider that the people who are usually called crazy are simply the first ones to try something new.

It wasn't long ago that no one was following my work. I almost deleted my Facebook fan page the night I created it because I was embarrassed since I had so few "Likes." I remember that some people who went to my high school even wrote Facebook statuses that read, "Jake Ducey invites you to like his page. YA RIGHT!!!"

At the time, hunger and stubbornness pushed me. I wanted to show those people what I was made of, but I was getting a lot of resistance. Someone even made a fake Facebook page and commented on every single picture and status on both my personal and professional pages, trying to slander my name and work. They said everything from "He didn't even write that book" to "He made the whole story up." These people also went so far as to send me private messages telling me that they wished I would die. They said that if they had it their way, I would've died when I flipped my car. They said I was going nowhere. That I should just give up, and that I was a fraud. . . .

I knew that these people must have been miserable with their own lives if they were willing to devote hours on end to comment on hundreds of my statuses and photos with a fake Facebook page. And friends told me that I was the talk of high school reunion parties with old high school mates. People would say, "Jake lost his mind. He's totally crazy. What an idiot." As much as these comments really hurt me, I kept going. I kept reminding myself of what Bob Marley said: "[I've] got a job to do and [I've] gotta fulfill that mission. . . ."

Then, my book launched and it hit the Amazon bestseller list within forty-eight hours. Old friends who once turned their backs on me began to send me Facebook messages to apologize and congratulate me. But the resistance didn't stop—death has still been wished upon me. I've been called a fraud. I've been told I couldn't write. I've been told I would fail. I've been told I look too stupid to be taken seriously. I've had people tell me I was a sellout because I was selling a book. And the list goes on. . . .

I even remember my best friend, Luke, asking, "Why do all these people follow you if all they do is talk shit to you?" I had no idea, but by then, I didn't really care. I didn't have the time to wonder. My mind was too focused on my vision and there's no time to switch the focus to what some person thinks of me, or why they're doing what they're doing. No time!

Today it's gotten to the point where I really, truly couldn't care less. The opinion you have of yourself is the only one you should care about. I've realized that we really do have to let the good outweigh the bad. Focus on the good and forget the bad, especially if you want to reach your fullest vision. When I reach my fullest vision there will probably be thousands of people who hate me before I die.

American speaker and author Byron Katie once said, "It's not your job to like me. It's mine." The easiest thing to do in life is to just say "no contest" and submit your dreams and freedom for a number in the line of conformity. Each person wants you to be like him or her because it's easier that way. It's much less challenging than having a bunch of people who look differently, think differently, believe different things, and awaken to a different sun. If people do this, then—oh no!—they would be on their own, which they already are. But for some reason we seem to forget this and, instead, we look for acceptance from a tribe or clan.

Tribes and clans are nothing more than brotherhoods of illusions where we hide from who we are to fit the customs that someone else made up. If we follow well enough, then we are well received and easily liked. Life becomes much easier—or, in reality, does it become that much harder?

We're all on the pursuit—of whatever it is that makes us happy. Most of us are looking to fall through the trapdoor, into a sea full of mermaids, where life is comfortable and easy. But life becomes a choking monotony when the reflection you see in the mirror is actually the face of everyone except yourself. An image that reflects the fact that you've allowed your life to be determined by the beliefs of others, because you thought it would make life easier.

Society is like a ritzy tennis club. Either you fit in and wear the pink collared shirt with your sweater tied around your neck or you are given so much resistance that you are either asked to leave or you leave on your own because you just can't fit in. Those who leave are the artists, the recluses, and the innovators—the ones who move society forward.

The Need for Security

We try to fit because we believe that it will bring us security. We think that if we give up who we are, we will be accepted by others. We assume that we will find refuge within the umbrella of the ordinary—unaware of the rain of death that awaits us there.

The only truth in life is that we're going to die. So how secure can life really be? Is it really worth spending all of our energy trying to fit the ideal of some Hollywood ad agency? You know the one with perfect tits, washboard abs, artificial smile, fake tan, and skinny legs? Hundreds of millions of us suck this bottle of superficiality. Ah, the corporate agenda, nothing like it—except dog shit, which has an eerily similar fragrance when stepped into. And the repugnant smell just stays with you.

Unless, of course, you decide what beauty and confidence is for yourself. It's a less secure path. You will have to be different.

And therefore, you will be questioned. But at least you will be yourself.

There are no oxygen masks to protect your lungs from breathing in the feces of a corrupt society. The only thing that can protect you is a silent whisper from your soul, a whisper that only you can hear. It's a faint echo that reverberates within the walls of your heart, which tells you what you should *really* do with your life, rather than what everybody else wants you to do.

But, you see, the government doesn't like that, and corporations don't like that, because then you may not buy all the things that you don't really need. *Well, you mustn't do that—you've got to live in a complicated way—get the kind of stuff that defines you as someone with social status.* I believe they tell us this because if we are insecure, we will not try to be the individuals that we really are—we will simply do what is considered acceptable and normal. And we become so unsure of ourselves that we try to validate the rules of society's game, criticize others, and try to make everyone else play the game along with us.

But you can't tell someone that they must play a game they don't want to play. You can't tell people that if they don't do what you want them to do, then they won't be accepted. It's only because we are unsure and scared that we conform. We wear the same clothes, look at images on billboards as references, do what is normal in school, and then get a high-paying career. But it's only a game, and you don't have to play (especially if you have something else in mind).

When you consider that there may be something else for you, the question becomes, *To eat shit and die, or to find something else and then die?* At least for a while, the world will look at you as if you were a hellish creature bound for the underworld if your goal is weirdness and uniqueness over conformity. One of the most important things to be aware of when choosing what you want to do with your life is that, either way, no matter whom you try to impress or what dreams you think you should give up on to be more well liked, you're still going to die. So why not live warmly, within the sweaty hands of risk, uncertainty, and individualism?

There are three kinds of junkies in this world (and I believe we all fall into one category): a junkie of substance (drugs, alcohol, and superficial, material things), a junkie of acceptance (one who conforms because it's the easiest way to never be questioned), and a junkie of risk (the least glamorized of the three, but the surest way to find yourself). Regardless of what you choose, you're either moving closer to who you are or further away from who you are.

Seeking Advice

"But I don't want to go among mad people," Alice remarked.

"Oh, you can't help that," said the Cat, "we're all mad here. I'm mad. You're mad."

"How do you know I'm mad?" said Alice.

"You must be," said the Cat, "or you wouldn't have come here."

—Lewis Carroll, *Alice's Adventures in Wonderland*

Life is either a daring adventure comprised of sheer uncertainty in the pursuit of finding yourself or it's a brutal risk of everything in the name of false hopes, such as safety and popularity. Our culture falsely promises us that if we only do what everyone else does— get the nine-to-five job, get the car, get the house, and whatever else they are selling these days—that we will be safe and happy. But the truth is that it doesn't matter which way you go. Eventually you are going to die. No one can promise you safety, so why not live the adventure and die along the way knowing you did what you wanted to do?

A lot of people have opinions about how you should live your life but don't even like their own lives. Forgive them anyway. They are only telling you what to do out of the fear that you will be different, and thus, cause them to question their own existence. Life is short and the thrill is found in the new and different, in not listening to other people's opinions. We listen because we want security, when in reality nothing is less secure than following the advice of people who are judging you.

Don't take advice from the wrong people. It's important to look at who we are listening to. Look to people who have what you want—whether it's health, happiness, wealth, relationships, and more. Really consider if the people who are giving you advice are the ones you really want advice from.

Ignoring Opinions

Today's mighty oak is just yesterday's nut that held its ground.

—David Icke, English writer, public speaker,
and former professional footballer

When you take a moment to think about most of the inventions that make our modern world more comfortable (airplanes, movies, radios, computers, phones, electricity, and more), you'll see that the inventors and their teams were generally regarded as crazy while creating their life's work. Steve Jobs, the Wright brothers, Walt Disney, Nikola Tesla, and Albert Einstein are just a few of the many iconic figures of today's world. They were also the *nuts* of yesterday.

In our modern world—through technological advances such as

the Internet—opinions, norms, and beliefs travel around the world in no time. As a result, we've been shaped to think and behave in certain ways because they are normal, cool, and acceptable. By looking at history, we see that following the norm has never made a large contribution to humanity. The ones who really make a difference are always the weirdos and the misfits.

By examining the thousands of human beings I've crossed paths with in this life, I can say that the happiest of them haven't been the normal, cool, and acceptable ones. They've always been at least a bit freakish (just like all the trendsetters, difference makers, and social revolutionaries).

We all want to be ourselves, don't we? We want to be happy. So let's do it! However, it's only possible if we are okay with being different, overcoming this fear, and doing it anyway. Start by asking the questions that really arouse your curiosity, dressing how you want to dress, doing what you want to do with your time, and examining where you're being too "realistic". . . . Are your beliefs ones you formed yourself, or are they ones that you accepted that were passed down by your parents, friends, or the media?

The Duty of Civil Disobedience

The revolution has always been in the hands of the young. The young always inherit the revolution.

—Huey Newton, African-American political and urban activist,
cofounder of the Black Panther Party

I would like to see more social emphasis on changing the status quo. I would like my news channels to report on things other than beheadings, car crashes, bombs, and reports on depression, inflation, and shootings. I would like to be controlled less, and not treated like a terrorist in my own country (been to the airport lately?). I would like the money that we call *tax*, the money that we have to pay or we are thrown in jail, to fund the local schools in our areas, not to fund dirty wars many of us wish to have no part in. I would like to see an immediate decrease in the enforcement of petty laws, and more focus to take money out of politics and voting, restrict corporate oppression and greed, and end the Federal Reserve. Most of all, I would like to be left alone by those who, in the names of democracy and freedom, monitor my e-mails, and do not use more of our taxes to benefit our communities. If this is what government does, then I don't want it.

Government can be contradiction that sucks the last dollars out of the working class, takes advantage of children in distant lands, funds war instead of education, and invades countries to supposedly instill peace, but instead loses its integrity more and more each instant. Or government can be a system that creates a more peaceful, and sustainable, world. But the paradox of politics today seems to be that it's supposed to be "by the people, for the people," yet in reality the government serves but a few people.

I am simply pointing out that genuine and legitimate problems are not being addressed (and that we as individuals now have the power to create change): people are aware of massive corporate and economic exploitation and nothing is being changed, the planet is being destroyed, teen suicide rates are off the charts, government officials argue so much that the government can't even stay open to keep a million people in their jobs, the division between social and economic classes grows every day, and poor people are exploited all around the world for resources. And what is even worse than the fact that this is all happening is the fact that these subjects are not being addressed.

The good news is that life has a lot more meaning when we stand for something. And right now we all can do this—make it a priority to help others, to share our individual talents, and ask questions. We must rise to the occasion. This is what creates a better world! Now I don't mean to awaken so many dead philosophers, but Emerson also said, "The antidote to this abuse of formal government is the influence of private character, and the growth of the individual."

Plain and simple—the world will get better when we all make an important part of our lives to become better people ourselves. When we do this, we see we are responsible for the future we create. This future can be improved when you . . .

Face your fears.
Speak up.
Meditate.
Have a vision.
Improve on your habits.
Help others.
Be caring.
Trust yourself.
Tie your work into giving back to your community.
Be your own authority.
Take risks to do what you love.

Never has it been a better time to get going on the aforementioned. You can almost feel the sense of urgency to create a better world! I feel it especially while reading author Paulo Coelho's outline of the human condition: "How can we be so arrogant? The planet is, was, and always will be stronger than us. We can't destroy it; if we overstep the mark, the planet will simply erase us from its surface and carry on existing. Why don't they start talking about not letting the planet destroy us?"

It's true that year after year we hear the same things, watch promises left unfilled, and see our hopes turn sour while the world continues to go down the drain—more wars, more poverty, more debt, more uncertainty, and more corruption. And people often ask, "Do you see *any* hope?" And the answer is that I see a world of it—it's just not in the Oval Office, and may never be. Change is not coming from anyone but the public—it is coming from you and me.

We don't need to wait for direction from "leaders." We have the ideas and the drive, and global communication is instantaneous. The "KONY 2012" movement showed us that your message has the potential to reach hundreds of millions of people in weeks. And revolutions have *already* occurred in places like the Middle East with the Arab Spring, and with the help of the Internet, messages of change, hope, and inspiration were exchanged.

Now is the time for us to rise up. What can you do today to make the world a better place? Start by doing what you love and sharing your gifts with the world. That is the greatest rebellion. Dedicate your life to making the world brighter and to your own self-discovery, rather than suffocating your creativity to memorize pointless facts, formulas, and definitions, or working at some place you're half-passionate about for forty years so you can retire comfortably and live out the remaining years of the life you mostly wasted.

Until this world of more justice comes, revolt. Show your gifts to the world and be giving. Use these gifts to improve the world. When you and I do this, when we do this together, we will be ready for a world of more justice, peace, and stability.

Chapter 13

The Inward Journey

The weak can never forgive. Forgiveness is the attribute of the strong.

—GANDHI

Imagine being imprisoned for over a quarter of a century, unjustly. This is what happened to Nelson Mandela on August 5, 1962, when police captured him. His life was taken away from him. He was convicted of conspiracy to overthrow the state, and sentenced to life imprisonment in South Africa. He was verbally and physically harassed by white prison wardens, and spent his days breaking rocks into gravel, until being reassigned a few years later to work in a lime quarry.

It's insane that such an incredible activist and human being was thrown into jail. He is someone who was capable of so much, and he had to spend his time breaking rocks. Can you imagine that happening to you?

Mandela was initially not allowed to wear sunglasses while working in the lime quarry, and the glare of the limes in the sun severely and permanently damaged his eyes. There's no way I would've been able to forgive people who did that to me, but Mandela said that resentment is like drinking poison, and then hoping you will kill your enemies with the poison. This was a guy who could hardly see, and yet he continued to study and use his time wisely while in prison. He remained an optimist. While in prison, knowing that he was sentenced for the rest of his life, he worked on his autobiography and studied in hopes that he would have another opportunity. He prepared himself for an opportunity that he couldn't even see.

His optimistic outlook is incredible, especially considering how alone he must have felt. He was hardly able to see any visitors when they came and their visits were highly infrequent. He didn't get to see his daughters for thirteen years, and yet he remained positive, even while imprisoned in the worst circumstances possible. Mandela focused on the beauty that was still available to him. He said that soccer made him feel alive and triumphant despite the horrible situation he was in. And this situation was bad. He ended up developing severe tuberculosis, was aggravated by the dark conditions in his solitary cell, lost part of his eyesight, missed his mother's and firstborn son's funerals, and spent twenty-seven years in prison. He was finally freed in 1990. Yet despite all of the horror that he had to endure, he forgave these people and stayed focused. He didn't let the pain or anger eat away at him. He didn't fuss with all the "would haves," "could haves," and "should haves." He didn't live in the past, but triumphed forward toward the future in the present.

Let's consider seeing him as an example—let's consider putting our pain into perspective. You may feel wronged, you may feel hurt, and you may feel taken advantage of. But by focusing on this and accepting that story, you are allowing yourself to be disempowered.

Mandela stayed focused the whole time he was in prison. He prepared himself, and as soon as he got out of jail he gave a speech to 100,000 people. I am blown away by the fact that he was able to stay positive and hopeful throughout that entire process. He said, "I am fundamentally an optimist. Whether that comes from nature or nurture, I cannot say. Part of being optimistic is keeping one's head pointed toward the sun, one's feet moving forward. There were many dark moments when my faith in humanity was sorely tested, but I would not and could not give myself up to despair. That way lays defeat and death."

This optimistic philosophy, which required a lot of forgiveness, led him to become one of the greatest activists and leaders in human history. It allowed him not only to let go of anger and stay peaceful when he was released, but it allowed him to free an entire country and change the world. And because of that, he eventually won the Nobel Peace Prize in 1993.

Would you be able to do what he did? If you feel that you aren't capable of this type of greatness, think again. Mandela was not a messiah. He felt that he was just an ordinary man who was in an extraordinary situation that rose up to the challenge. You too are being challenged in your life, and you too have the same capabilities to forgive whoever has wronged you, and to forgive yourself.

You must proceed forward even when you don't know what's promised because, like Nelson Mandela said, "There is no passion to be found in playing small, in settling for a life that's less than the one you are capable of living." So if you feel someone is bringing resistance to your life, don't fight against him or her. It's only going to paralyze you. It's only going to tighten up your body. Instead, look at it as an opportunity to practice kindness and forgiveness because in the process, you are going to inspire people, free yourself to make a bigger difference, and be happier and more fulfilled.

We have all faced pain. I am sure you have been hurt and wronged at some point, but now is the time to let all of that go, to gain something bigger. As soon as you can let that go, there's something bigger that life will present to you. So let it go. And remember that forgiveness is the alchemy that can change your soul into gold. It's going to return the possibilities to your spirit. Let the possibilities return, and forgive.

Keystone XL

> True forgiveness is when you can say, "Thank you for that experience."
>
> —Oprah Winfrey

I was prisoner number fifty-nine, and this is my story: I flew from San Diego to Washington, D.C., in 2013 to peacefully protest in front of the White House against bringing to light one of the darkest shadows still within the earth. That shadow is in a place most of us will never go—Alberta, Canada. Alberta is home to forests that cover sludgy bitumen beneath the ground that can be refined into Canadian Tar Sands Oil, at the expense of precious land, tons of clean water, and the releasing of one of the largest carbon reserves on the planet. And it's all to create the Keystone XL Oil Pipeline.

This is why I went to protest against multinational corporations bringing it into sight for profit. And that's why the government detained sixty-four of us without charging us with a crime, reading us our rights, or letting us see a judge (regardless of the fact that we had a legal permit obtained by 350.org). But that, of course, was irrelevant because President Obama has made it legal for the

Secret Service to arrest anyone, without charging him or her with a crime, if they are present at a protest that the government doesn't find pleasing for any reason.

The night before our protest, we sat in an old community building, listening to one of the Obama administration's widely quoted climatologists, Jim Hansen, who said that if humans expect to mitigate or slow global warming, coal must be phased out by 2030. "If the tar sands are thrown into the mix, it is essentially game over for the climate," Hansen warned.

Despite these facts, many people desire an awakening of this monster—the Keystone XL Oil Pipeline—including Exxon and TransCanada. These companies were proposing an extension of the tar sands oil into the United States. We wanted to stop this, so the next day we were thrown in jail, while Obama vacationed at Martha's Vineyard.

Prior to our arrest, 350.org told us to expect a fine for the action, as it is consistent with a minor traffic violation. Instead, I was put in a Secret Service police van and held for almost three days without being read my rights or charged with a crime. Quickly, productive discussion among detainees emerged. We played spontaneous games where we yelled out our favorite inspirational quotes at the top of our lungs for hours—a deep sense of solidarity formed among us.

While all of this took place, there was also a lot of pain and discomfort. Six people were hospitalized because we were not given sufficient amounts of water. Six ounces of water every twelve hours in the smoldering humidity of the Washington, D.C., jail cells wasn't enough, especially when the guard forgot (or so he said) to bring us some for almost an entire day.

In my cell, I was just inches below a massive fluorescent light that made me woozy in combination with the limited amount of water I'd been able to drink. Within the first eighteen to twenty-four hours the guards began splitting all the protesters up, sending us through the night to other jails, because they said that ours was full (even though it wasn't). On our way back from checking out a new jail, which they told us was also full, I told a guard that I had to use the bathroom. He told me that I had to wait until I got into my new cell in another jail we were headed to. But I couldn't go in a cell, the toilets were right next to the faces of our cellmates. I didn't tell him that, I just said I had to go, immediately.

Upon hearing this he led me downstairs. It was filthy. I went while countless inmates who probably committed real crimes watched me. My dignity had been violated somewhere between the filthy floors (I wondered if they'd ever been cleaned) and my inability to move my arms or legs outside of the range of movement the cuffs permitted. "It's a white boy," one inmate yelled while I finished up using the bathroom.

Back in the police van, I watched people's spirits being broken by my own government right before my eyes. Many complained that they needed medical treatment, but the guards didn't listen. I remember trying to encourage an older man to stay strong while we sat there, sweating, with our arms and legs cuffed. He couldn't. I could see the life in his eyes fading. He was miserable and uncomfortable. He was overheated, dehydrated, and afraid.

While they drove us to another jail cell, a fellow detainee spoke passionately about how the extraction of the tar sands involves clear-cutting and scraping away all forests and possible life, often one hundred feet down. By maneuvering massive machines with billowing smokestacks and steel-toothed scoops, the companies would wage war with the land. When the thick black slush is spooned out of its 300-million-year-old home, hundreds of toxic chemicals await to separate, to be thinned and thickened into a more marketable sludge.

How could this be happening when, at his own inauguration, President Obama promised environmentalists (who helped him receive the opportunity to stand on that podium) that he would take care of Mother Earth? He promised that, "This was the moment when the rise of the oceans began to slow and our planet began to heal." Yet instead of protecting the planet and letting others do so peacefully, there we sat, indefinitely detained for wanting to stop an environmental disaster that *Obama* wanted to enact, without being read our Miranda rights, or even knowing what our charges were.

The horrid pattern of moving from jail to jail, and sitting in concrete cells, continued for the entire three days. And all the while my hands and feet were never uncuffed. On the last day, we patiently awaited our court hearing (or so we thought), and then they let us all go, without charging us with anything, or even telling us what had happened.

When we were outside of jail we found out about the number of us that had been hospitalized from the severe conditions. "How the heck could I forgive anyone for that?" I said to my best friend after telling him the story back in Los Angeles, having just landed from Washington, D.C. I was beyond pissed off. My veins pulsed with hatred, not only because of what had happened, but because I found out firsthand that they really can do whatever they want, and get away with it, whenever they want (which is almost all the time). I sat on his patio by the pool, face-first in the concrete, crying like a little kid, barely resisting punching the ground as if it were President Obama himself and his advisers, who had most likely called for our detainment from a beautiful brunch at Martha's

Vineyard overlooking a garden that cost millions of dollars while thousands couldn't even afford breakfast in Washington, D.C. It was the deepest hatred I ever felt in my life toward anything or anyone. "How could I forgive them?" I repeated.

I didn't know how, but I knew I had to, or it would eat me up inside forever. I knew that if I didn't forgive, I would never be, as Henry David Thoreau said, "a counter-friction to stop the machine." I didn't know then that our deep hatred and unhandled rage, however warranted, never serves us in creating a better world—never. What I did know, however, is that I couldn't write well with so much angst. I knew that I couldn't share this story effectively if I was still too angry.

I sat there back in Los Angeles, still crying, recalling the trauma and the general heartbreak I felt. I realized that in America, we don't actually live in the land of the free. "And then they did this . . ." I continued to explain what happened to my friend Cole.

"I know it sucked, man. But when are you going to stop?" he said. That's when I realized something—they win if I can't forgive them. And that's what they want: a bunch of pissed-off people who can't handle their emotions. They don't want us calm. If we were, we would find solutions to rise above their failing systems of government and commerce.

I could feel all the stress in my body. This helped me see, very clearly, that we're never free from what has happened to us if we can't realize (however hard it is) that people do what they do because it's where they are in life. We all have different values, and it's our values that produce our actions. The government values economic growth and control. As a result, they are willing to detain innocent people to stop protests that could halt millions of dollars' worth of oil production, even if it can destroy the environment.

While I, on the other hand, have different values—I value the health of our planet.

Forgiveness is the act of accepting others just as they are today, even if you don't agree with the way they are living their lives or with what they have done. Forgiveness is the ability to ask, "What did I learn from this? How can I feel empowered from what has happened?" It is not focusing on how you were wronged.

I am grateful that I learned how strong I am. I learned that I can be extremely strong, especially when it's the only choice I have. I also learned that there were sixty-three other people who were also willing to lose their freedom to ensure the freedom of the rest of the nation. That inspires me, and I am grateful to have experienced it.

While in the cells, I knew I couldn't physically fight back. That option only leads to your being killed or locked up. But what I can do is fight back with creativity. I can free people through writing, speaking, and unparalleled work ethic. Knowing this helped settle my rage and helped me forgive them. We must channel our anger into creative expression and persistent action.

English novelist George Orwell said, "In a time of universal deceit, telling the truth is a revolutionary act." But I would add that the real revolutionary act is to forgive, release our anger, keep fighting, and rise up against the power structures—to claim our freedoms and planet back. This is the belief that has brought me to where I am today.

Forgive Yourself

Generally, when we think of forgiveness, we think of forgiving things outside of ourselves—other people, past experiences, and times that we feel we have been wronged. In a physical world where everything is based on the perception of our senses and what we see, we often forget about what we feel inside. We forget that so much happens internally, and we get mad and frustrated with ourselves. And later, we forget to forgive ourselves, which leaves feelings and experiences lingering in our memories that cause us to think less of ourselves.

There is an ancient Hawaiian practice, a mantra, called "Ho'oponopono." It means, "I'm sorry, I love you, please forgive me." "I'm sorry, I love you, please forgive me." Isn't that beautiful?

Personally, when I think of that, I immediately think of forgiving somebody else. I think about asking someone else for forgiveness, the universe for forgiveness, or Mother Earth for forgiveness. But what I am inviting you to consider is offering that to yourself. "I love you, I am sorry, please forgive me." Not to anyone else, right now, just to yourself.

"I love you, I am sorry, please forgive me."

We're so focused on being good in other people's eyes. We forgive other people, ask them for forgiveness, and tell them that we are sorry, when really we serve the world best when we forgive ourselves. We have to stop beating ourselves up and bagging on ourselves. Yes, you may have messed up. Yes, you may have done something wrong. But you are learning. You are only here for a little while, so why spend your life resenting yourself and behaviors or characteristics you have? Why hate the way you look, the things you've done, who you've kissed, the way you've failed, or the way you've acted? It's over. It's done and there is nothing that you can do except say, "I am sorry, I love you, please forgive me."

Forgive yourself. You are doing the best that you can. You weren't trying to mess up. You weren't trying to make your past terrible. You weren't trying to hurt anyone else. You weren't trying to mess up your life. You weren't trying to let people down.

And you certainly weren't trying to let yourself down. So accept all of this. Accept that you were doing the best you could, and that you still are doing the best that you can. Accept that, if you really want to serve other people, if you really want to serve the world, and if you really want to be fulfilled and happy, you must forgive yourself and let it go.

Try to be like a dog. One, two, three—drop it. One, two, three—drop it. Let it go. It's over. It's done. There is nothing you can do now. You messed up. But did you learn from it? If so, great, that's all that matters. Did you see where you could improve next time? Perfect, do better next time.

We all mess up. I messed up in the process of releasing my first book, and there have been times when I've pissed a lot of people off. And I am supposed to be this happy-go-lucky kid, but sometimes I get pissed off at people. Sometimes my ego gets the best of me.

Remember the story about the promotional video for my first book? The one that wasn't accepted by a site and my publicist believed that it was because the company was jealous of the video? That really pissed me off, especially because I knew that my intention with the creation of the video was to help and inspire people. I looked at the other videos on the blog and I believed that mine had a lot more intention in it. I said I was sorry to the president of that company, but what I really needed to do was forgive myself.

When you make a mistake and upset someone, or let them down, you start to be hard on yourself. "I'm such an idiot. Why did I do that? I'm such an asshole. I'm such a bad person. Blah, blah, blah, blah, blah . . ." And the mind goes on forever. So if you want to make the world a better place and you want to be happier, forgive yourself. You are only human and you are doing the best that you can. The nicest people in the world make mistakes. Even Gandhi made mistakes.

When Gandhi's wife was sick, he wouldn't let her use Western medicine and she died. Gandhi did this! He is supposed to be this beautiful saint, but because he wouldn't let his wife get medicine, she died. Then, he got sick shortly after and took the Western medicine. That's not acting in integrity. But that is being human. We're not always going to be right, we're not always going to be perfect. Accept it.

"I'm sorry, I love you, please forgive me." Go to the mirror and say that while looking into your eyes—go into your heart and say it to yourself. Ask yourself for forgiveness. Tell yourself that you love you, that you're sorry, and that you were trying the best that you could. Realize that you were doing the best that you could, and you're going to continue to do all you can to continue to grow.

When you can forgive yourself, you release the burden and you free other people. You smile bigger, your face is wider, and your body is lighter. You have more energy to pursue your work, your mission in life, and to help other people. You're going to fail, you're going to make mistakes, and you're going to get pissed at yourself. Forgiveness is the act of restoring your possibilities.

When you're mad or upset with yourself, you immediately limit the possibilities of who you are. Forgive yourself, love yourself, and tell yourself that you do. If you don't, nobody will. Nobody can do this for you—you have to do it yourself.

So whatever it is, stop right now and think about it. Think about where you messed up, the person you think you hurt, the situation you think you messed up, who you think you let down, or where you think that you're not being true to yourself, and just forgive yourself. At least you're aware of it. And now do the best you can to move forward, to take the next step, and if you fall again, just get back up.

Measure your character not by how you fail, but by how many

times you get back up, and by how many times you can keep putting the faith back in yourself. Recognize the amount of times that
you restore the possibilities of who you are. Forgive yourself. It's
the only choice you have if freedom is what you want.

Self-Love

> Your problem is you're . . . too busy holding on to your
> unworthiness.
>
> —Ram Dass, American contemporary spiritual teacher

Sometimes you just need to look at yourself in the mirror and say, "I
love you so much. Thank you! Thank you!" Unfortunately, we live
in a world that promotes the opposite. "Are you skinny enough?"
asks the cover of the tabloids. "Do you have strong enough abs?"
"Look at how smart *this* person is!"

The media gives us thousands of reasons to reflect on our own
insecurities. A world has been built around us that oozes insecurity,
uncertainty, and self-hatred. People literally kill themselves because
they love the same sex and it's not accepted. They are so upset with
who they are, because society has told them that it is unacceptable,
that they think ending their life is the solution. Others starve themselves to death to fit the twenty-first-century consensus of what it
means to be beautiful, while others spend thousands of dollars on
college, but never get the grades they are capable of because they
don't think they are smart enough. The list is endless.

Why do we do this? I don't have all the answers, but I don't
think it matters. Asking yourself *why* simply drives you crazy.
"Why am I not good enough, not pretty enough, not succeeding,
too fat, too insecure?" Ask yourself questions like these and the

mind will give you a million reasons. Ask, and you receive. But instead of belaboring over why, look for solutions. Ask *how*. Ask, "How can I improve this?"

How can you love yourself more? By focusing on the little things. Focus on what you do during the ordinary hours of the day. This is the determining factor in how our beliefs are structured about who we are and what we're capable of accomplishing.

Here are some questions and suggestions to consider:

1. Do you eat to give yourself nutrients, or do you eat just to feel gratified for a bit? If it's the latter, you're probably eating to cover up deeper emotions that you are not dealing with. And this is probably causing dissatisfaction with yourself, but you don't always realize it because you continue to nibble instead of occasionally sitting still.

2. Fill in the blank: "I am _____." What were the first adjectives to come to mind? Earlier in the book I explained that you can tell a lot about a person's inner state by the adjectives they use. (Personally, I filled in the blank with "I am powerful, I am sexy, I am a smart and capable.") How about you? What did you fill in the blank with? If your adjectives were less than ideal, then take a few moments to consciously choose new ones and practice writing them down to ingrain your mind with a different thought pattern.

3. What do you do when you look in the mirror? Do you immediately look for every fault on your face?

Instead, try telling yourself that you love who you are. (Yes, it will be uncomfortable if you've never done it before, but do it anyway!)

"Mirror" Exercise

Take two to five minutes and stand in front of the mirror, closely. Look into your own eyes, and begin to compliment yourself. Start with the things that you love that others say about you from time to time. Notice your face. Notice your body. Notice your personality. Compliment yourself. Let each compliment sink in for a second, and keep going. This is a great exercise, if you commit to it. It helps you get into a more confident emotional state in just a few moments. Experiment by practicing it every morning for a week.

Inner Beauty

Beauty is how you feel inside, and it reflects in your eyes. It is not something physical.

—Sophia Loren, actress

I used to worry a bit about the fact that I didn't have the educational credentials to write. I never got higher than a C in an English class, and I got a score of 1470 out of 2400 on my SATs. Other people didn't take me very seriously. A lot of people told me that I needed to study writing in college before trying to write a book. We all face doubts that question how amazing and beautiful we are, but you have to just say to yourself, *Look, I know I'm beautiful. And so I am going to proceed from that place, because I am beautiful, capable, smart, and so much more. . . .*

Once we get scared or self-conscious, it's easy to get lost in trying to appear like something we're not, trying too hard to be perfect, or worrying about our hair, clothes, shoes, teeth, skin, muscles, and stomach. I even notice myself getting caught up in trying to perceive the image that someone else has of me—I wonder how they feel about what I'm wearing, saying, how I look, or what I am doing. I try to figure out what words they would use to define me. But I'll never figure it out, and if I do, it doesn't even matter.

The more we wonder, the more we get lost. We must remember that the dream we have within ourselves of who we are is the only image that's important. The image that you have in your imagination about who you are, what you want to be, and what you want to represent is all that matters.

You may be fretting about what you look like or how you sound. Yes, our world is often based on how we appear and what we do. It is, but the truth is that we're *beautiful* when we remember that we're beautiful to begin with. It sounds cliché, but that's only because it's true.

When we know that we're beautiful, we don't need anyone's approval. When we don't need anyone to tell us, all of a sudden everyone tells us how beautiful we are. I promise that whether you think you are beautiful or not, just stop for the rest of the day and get in touch with the possibility that you are. You're a possibility. You're a possibility of beauty. Get in touch with the meaning of that statement, feel how that feels, and be okay if you fail at believing it. If you think it for long enough, you will eventually succeed. People will start to say, "Wow, look at that." You'll catch people's eyes because you'll be transmitting beautiful self-confidence.

Beauty is not based on whether or not you have a six-pack, or the perfect butt or boobs. We all know there are tons of people who've changed the world who don't fit that stereotype. Be in touch with your inner beauty and the world will start to recognize it.

Your beauty is not tangible. It's not your body. It's a feeling that moves you. A feeling that inspires you and brings you confidence. It's a feeling that isn't based on external appearances, but on inner feelings. The outer world is secondary. The color of your skin, the way you wear your hair, the color of makeup that you buy, and the cologne that you wear won't make a difference if you don't feel good inside. Besides, beauty is subjective and you will never be considered the most beautiful to all of your beholders. But if you transmit confidence, strength, and inner beauty, people—the right people—will gravitate toward you and respect the love that you carry from within. And when this happens, all the little imperfections that you wanted to change can become parts of yourself that you accept and love.

When you're connected to yourself and assured of your beauty, all the fear melts away and you turn into a giant puddle of beauty. You become a beautiful mess. The fears and doubts and the "I wish I would've turned out like this . . ." will never stop. But what you can do is connect to the beauty within.

Get into a space within yourself that allows you to know you're beautiful. And when you do this be aware that some people won't like it and they'll be sure to let you know that or ask you to change. So other voices in your head will say, *Oh . . . wait . . . you're not this. And you don't have the credentials* . . . and it will go on and on forever.

We all go crazy as our minds try to force us to become some

perfect version of ourselves that can't and won't exist. And I know it's hard to fight the mind. But this is why we have to train our minds to see our beauty and worth. You may forget how beautiful you are at times, but when you do, just remember that feeling that lies between your in-breath and your out-breath. The moment when you stop and you're not thinking about anything. It's in that space, when you are connected to that feeling that you find your beauty. That's where you find the true you.

Self-Respect

> Self-respect is a question of recognizing that anything worth having has a price.
>
> —Joan Didion, American author

Self-respect is one of the most important qualities a human can obtain, and it is gained by having higher standards. You must have standards for what and who you let into your life in everything from who you are romantic with, to where you work, what you do with your time, and how you treat your body. You must set standards. When you increase your standards, you increase your level of self-respect.

If something is stressful and negative in your life, you should probably get it out of your experience if at all possible. If it's not up to the standards that you want—if it's not working for you—then don't be afraid to get rid of it. It's super-simple; if you want your life to have meaning, then you need to find it in different areas of your life.

Setting Standards High
(No Matter What)

Let us be about setting high standards for life, love, creativity, and wisdom. If our expectations in these areas are low, we are not likely to experience wellness. Setting high standards makes every day and every decade worth looking forward to.

—Greg Anderson, author

One day I was running on the beach where I live in San Diego. I had finished, and felt tired. I sat down after jumping in the ocean and I was thinking to myself about how tired I was. Then, out of the corner of my eye, somebody ran past me. I stopped and looked at him—it was a man who had two prosthetic legs. He was moving really fast, running past me, and I sat there and looked at him. I noticed the standard that he had set for himself and for his potential. I was blown away. In that moment, I realized how often we let our minds talk us into being more "realistic." We often justify our own mediocrity.

It doesn't matter whether you have a disability or a disease, fail a lot, or don't feel smart, capable, or ready—the first step for you to take is to decide who you are going to be, and what you want to do with your time.

Say No

Being unable to say no can make you exhausted, stressed, and irritable.

—Auliq Ice, author

In a world where so much of life is based on pleasing other people, being a nice person, and helping others, we often forget to say *no*. It's a magic word. You cannot say *yes* to everything. On the journey to fulfillment, it is very important not to overextend yourself. Yes, we must step out of our comfort zones and challenge ourselves, but we mustn't say yes to everything—we simply don't have the time.

Focus on what you do best and help people by doing so. If you're working on a goal and have certain things that are the most important things to you, you have to say no to other things that aren't in alignment with that. Sometimes this is really hard. But if you know it is not aligned with your biggest vision or goal, you may even need to say no to a family member or friend. Sometimes this is necessary so you can put more time into yourself, and into working on what you do best. Or perhaps you need to say no because you need downtime—don't feel bad about this. Time to relax, recuperate, and do nothing is really important for reaching your goals.

Saying no is a practice of self-love and discipline. No one should get upset with you when you are creating boundaries, and if they do, it will be short-lived. You can't live your life bending over backward for others all the time (even if you love to help people). Giving yourself self-time is essential to your well-being. It is the only way to feel full and have the ability to offer this fullness to other people.

Meditate

I'd like to be more patient! I just want everything now. I've tried to meditate, but it's really hard for me to stay still. I'd like to try to force myself to do it, because everybody says how wonderful meditation is for you, but I can't shut my mind up. So patience and learning is the key.

—Ellen DeGeneres, American comedian

Lately, I've had a lot going on with work and sometimes it can be difficult to manage other aspects of my life. It's difficult to get things done without feeling like they create total stress and drudgery. I know that if I didn't meditate every morning and night, I would probably burn out, get sick, and get nothing done. I meditate because there is an infinite source of creativity and consciousness, which is the driving force behind this reality, our thoughts, and the energy that sustains us. Who wouldn't want to connect with all of that? If you are thinking, *Nah, sounds boring! I'd rather watch television than do that*, then I invite you to consider that meditation may be exactly what you need to bring success and fulfillment into your daily life.

Here are three reasons to meditate:

1. Meditation helps your nervous system rest. There's no denying that we live in a fast-paced world that quickens each day. It seems like almost everyone is always stressed out. Our nervous systems are overstimulated with the busyness and stress from our to-do lists. This lifestyle is too much for our nervous systems and is part of the reason why we get diseases and become unhappy. Focusing on your breath in silence (meditation) gives you an opportunity to find a point of stillness. Doing so boosts your physical vitality and immune system because you balance out the overstimulation that you are exposed to each day.

2. Meditation sparks creativity. Every time that I am patient enough to stop and mull over my ideas, projects, and life, great ideas come to me. I believe that this is because the day is usually going so fast that it's hard to think creatively when there are so many little things to get done. This is why I believe that we should stop to meditate on our work.

3. Meditation time is *your* time. There's no right or wrong way to meditate. In fact, it's the practice of moving beyond the idea that things are right or wrong. It's time that you have for yourself so that you don't have to worry about the pressure of meeting someone's expectations or judgments. It's a time that allows you to be totally free. And the more you experience this sense of freedom, the more you will incorporate it into daily life.

I hope that you are convinced that meditation is worth a try. Here are three meditation tips to help you get started:

1. Don't overthink it—you're not doing it wrong. The point of meditation is to observe, and hopefully lessen, the constant chatter in your mind. Don't get stuck judging yourself about whether or not you are doing it right. If you have these thoughts, simply observe them and let them pass on by like clouds in the sky. Even if you have a lot going on in your mind, it's okay. Just be aware of what you are thinking and how you feel and don't get stuck in any thought or emotion.

2. Be comfortable. Sit in a comfortable position, with your spine straight, body relaxed, and your breath free. But if you prefer to lie down, that's okay too. As long as you close your eyes and focus on your breath, you are meditating. I suggest breathing slow deep breaths. Try breathing in for five seconds and out for five seconds, and repeating this cycle for five to ten minutes. If today you can only do one minute, that's okay too. Start small and work your way up.

3. Just do it. Often we don't try things because we think we don't know how. But, like I said before, there's no right way to meditate. It's just about trying it out and using your intuition to see what works best for you. However, this only comes with practice. So just do it! Try to meditate right now if you have a minute. You will notice the benefits and once you give it a try I am sure you will stick with it. It is a great way to connect with yourself and get in tune with who you truly are and what you truly want.

Chapter 14

Communication for Freedom

*Communication is the solvent of all problems and is
the foundation for personal development.*

—PETER SHEPHERD

Solon, an Athenian lawmaker, decreed shrinking from controversy
a crime. This is because he knew that if one does not clear their
feelings, the feelings control them and limit them from experiencing what is presently occurring in their life. I always knew this
conceptually, but really understood the true meaning of this concept when it happened to me.

Over the last four years I've been isolated from most people,
especially women, largely because I've been obsessively focused on
building my career. So it should've been no surprise that when I
finally fell in love (for the first time in my life) I would be head
over heels. I met a girl and we really connected. Then, she left for
the other side of the world to work for six months. Recently she let
me know that she met someone else and that she was moving to

Europe with him. Since I hadn't seen her for quite some time I had also connected with other people, but I still thought of her often and had hoped that maybe we would explore being together when she returned. So when she told me this, it really affected me. Then, a few weeks later I realized that part of the reason I felt so bad was because I felt disrespected and unappreciated because of the way she let me know that we should stop communicating—she told me in a Facebook message.

I know that I create my own feelings, but that doesn't take away the fact that the last thing she said to me before she left for work was, "I feel like I want to fall in love all over again. . . ." So yes, I felt even more disrespected when she explained that she was sending the Facebook message from home. We were in the same town and she was too busy to bring closure to the time we spent together. "Hey I met someone and we're moving to Europe. Hope we're all good. I am pretty busy so not much time though I am in town . . ." she wrote. The fact that she was home and wouldn't take the time to tell me this in person made me feel really awful. I felt like I had made the stupidest decision of my life by trying to make a difference in her life.

In response to her note I simply wrote that I appreciated all the time we had spent together and that I was grateful for it. She never acknowledged my words, which made me feel even worse. I showed a few friends our conversation and they were surprised. "Sometimes love is tough. You've got to tell her how you really feel or it will always be on your mind," one of my best friends said. I didn't listen to him and instead I spent the next week thinking about what had happened over and over again. By this time, I wasn't even upset that she met someone else anymore—that's just part of life. I just felt really disrespected.

I had really wanted to see her and bring our relationship to a real closure because that following Saturday I was giving a TED Talk to a thousand people (which is the biggest event I've ever done in my entire life). I didn't want to be at that event carrying those feelings. Not surprisingly, however, I never heard from her about getting together. The morning before my talk I woke up at 5:00 a.m. and my mind immediately starting thinking about her. So I decided to write to her about how I felt, which felt *really* good. By doing that, I felt that I was releasing many pent-up emotions that I'd been carrying around for two weeks. I was able to explain to her how unappreciated I felt, and how I knew that if I didn't share my feelings, I would not be honoring myself. It would be demonstrating a lack of self-love.

Throughout this process, I realized that if you don't share how you really feel, your feelings control you. Even if your life is busy and you don't consciously think about what upsets you, your buried thoughts and emotions torture your subconscious mind. Some thoughts and feelings don't just disappear with time; you need to take the initiative and clear them out.

Many of us live a limited version of our lives because we are filled with emotions from the past that were never released. We are told that it is mature to suck it up—that it's too childish to let someone know how we feel. If your intention is to hold yourself back from being all that you can be, then don't express your emotions. But if your intention is to grow and be who you really are, you must express yourself.

Our actions in life either come from a place of self-love or a place of self-hatred. *I don't hate myself*, you may think. But, although you may not hate yourself consciously, holding all those old emotions inside of yourself is an act of self-sabotage. And you may not even realize that you're doing this. Many times, our emotions have been bottled up for so long that we don't even know that they are there. But if you really stop and observe your actions, you may notice that you get madder or sadder or are taking things more personally than necessary in certain situations. If this ever happens to you, it's a good sign that you are holding onto old stuff.

You cannot be free until you let this old stuff go. And to let it go, you must express how you really feel. However, letting go and expressing doesn't always need to happen with words. Completely letting go of relationships that don't make you feel appreciated is another great way to clear space and honor how you truly feel. (Or at least let the other person know that you don't feel valued and find out if they have the capacity to change.)

When you stay in relationships that don't make you feel valued or respected, and don't say anything about it, you are showing your subconscious mind that you don't think that you are that important. You are demonstrating that you aren't worthy of better relationships, that you aren't special, and that this is the best you can receive (among other self-deprecating beliefs).

"Releasing Emotions" Exercise

Take a few minutes right now and think of all the unresolved conflicts, relationships, and emotions that you have stored inside of you. Is there someone you've wanted to say something to for a long time, but haven't? Is there past trauma or pain you tried to just move through, but still lingers? You've got to release it! Give it a try, because you will feel so much freer.

Now, write a letter to anyone you feel angst, anger, pain, upset, and/or heartbreak toward. Let them know that you appreciate them and that you also appreciate how you feel. This exercise will help even if the reader doesn't send the letter. Sometimes it may not be wise to actually contact the person one is writing to. Or sometimes that person has died. The powerful thing about this exercise is that even if you can't give it to them or they are dead, it's still an opportunity to release resentments.

Letting Go

Sometimes you love something, and it's not what you're meant to give all your love to. Maturity is the ability to recognize that there is a bigger picture beyond your individualistic concerns of where you want your love to go. Sometimes you just have to drop it.

When you feel heartbreak, it opens up the space to let more love and new possibilities in. I decided to share what had happened to me with the woman I was in love with, but letting you and other people know about my disheartening experience is scary. I shared this information in a blog shortly after it happened, but that was also really scary. I was so afraid that people would judge me but, regardless, I decided to feel this fear and allow myself to feel free from the pain that I *thought* she had caused me. When I shared this information on my blog, it was the most well-received blog post that I have ever written in my life. When we are vulnerable and put ourselves in uncomfortable situations, magic happens.

I am sure that your life hasn't been perfect, and that you've encountered challenges and felt pain that you didn't want others to know about. But it's not going to set you free to hide it. As soon as you understand that there is something to learn from what happened to you, incredible things begin to occur.

I went on a great writing streak when the whole episode happened with the girl I loved, and a few weeks later, I realized that I was in the flow for another book. I contacted my agent and let him know that I was writing another book (which is the book you are reading right now), and in only a few short months, the book was finished. By really stepping into my pain, a whole new possibility opened up. If I hadn't fallen in love with someone and they hadn't let me know they were in love with someone else, this book would never have been written.

Think for a moment about how many relationships end leaving both people feeling like they got the short end of the stick. And, afterward, neither of the people in the relationship releases their feelings of rejection and disappointment. This doesn't only happen in relationships, it may also happen if we don't reach a goal or we fall short on our dreams. Yeah, it sucks. But it sucks way less when you don't continue to hold a grudge. Doing so is not healthy. Holding your emotions inside is cancerous.

Be vulnerable with your emotions. If you want to free yourself, let people know! The only way you can release your pain is by sharing it, writing about it, vocalizing it, and being vulnerable. Your confidence increases to the amount of depth that you allow yourself to be vulnerable.

Pain isn't bad. We all feel pain. Pain is just as poetic as love. Progress comes not only from growth but also from destruction. Love comes not only from physical intimacy but also from the distant admiration and respect to let that person or situation go. Life is not only about success but also about discomfort and rejection. Consider that something may look bad in your life right now, or something that happened in your past may look negative, but it is really just a nudge to practice emotional detachment.

One day relatively soon, we are going to be gone. We will all be stripped of our lovers and memories—it will all disappear. So enjoy it all while you have it. And when experiences are over and people are gone, appreciate what you had. Thank the person you are holding a grudge against, or the situation you are holding a grudge against. Nothing is really yours—it's just yours to share and experience.

Listening to Others

When communicating with others, listening is really important. The more you listen, the more others will want to be around you. And the more you listen to others, the more they will trust you. When you listen, you increase other people's confidence in you and they will notice that you are listening, which makes them feel more valuable and honored. You can also learn a lot if you listen.

Here are four tips for listening:

1. Pause before replying to someone for about three to five seconds. By pausing you ensure that you are not interrupting the other person. You also show the other person that you're giving careful consideration to their words and you hear the other person better.
2. Ask questions to clarify what the other person has said. Never assume that you understand what someone is saying. If you have any doubt, ask, "What do you mean exactly?"
3. Paraphrase the speaker's words in your own words. After you finish listening say, "So you're saying . . . [and repeat their words back to them]." This will help you clarify whether or not you have understood them correctly. And it shows others that you care.

4. Nod your head when you follow what the speaker is saying, instead of talking over them. It's simpler, and it shows the speaker that you're engaged.

Spicing Up Conversations

Do you ever feel like your conversations are boring? Do you long for more connection in conversations with others? Would you like sixteen questions that will get most anyone to sound interesting, and maybe even become interested in you?

Here's my depiction of the average daily conversation:

"Hey, how are you?"
"Good. And you?"
"Good. What's new?"
"Not that much. How about you?"
"Kind of the same. Did you see the new *Breaking Bad* episode?"

Then, our conversations spiral out of control into a downward descent of nothingness from there on in. While we generally chit-chat about things that are meaningless, I believe that deep down we all want to have meaningful, real, authentic conversations. The challenge is that we are so used to routine conversations that we stay safe and hide our vulnerability.

To get out of these connection-cutting habits, I suggest that you try not to ask people how they are doing. We're so conditioned to it that I catch myself doing it, but whether it's a stranger, a friend, or a beautiful woman I've never before spoken with, I try to never say, "How are you?" It's too normal and ordinary. If you want to interest or touch anybody, then you've got to give him or her an experience that's out-of-the-ordinary, or they will just forget it.

Sometimes I pretend that I am a beautiful, tan woman with golden hair falling to my shoulders. And when I do this, I ask myself, "If a guy approached me and just asked me *how I was doing*, what would I (a wondrously beautiful woman of extraordinary splendor) think?" I would think that he was too boring and not good enough to even be worth the time of carrying on our conversation, let alone entertaining me. (I would probably be a cranky woman.) So I continue to pretend to be a woman like this and I ask myself, *what would really interest me?* (Try doing this exercise yourself and see what you learn.)

You can also use this technique to prepare for an interview. Imagine you are being interviewed for a job. Imagine walking into the room and instead of asking, "How are you?" you admit to them that you're nervous. Tell them how you feel. If you do, you immediately build a connection with them by bringing them into your experience. Or perhaps you are not nervous. Start by asking one of the following questions:

1. What has been the most interesting or best part of your day today? (This will get them thinking in a positive and out-of-the box way.)
2. What are you excited about in your life? (This will have them subconsciously associate positivity with you, because when people talk about what excites them, they will be left with the vibration of it.)

If you can get your potential boss to think differently or feel inspired by you, then you will have won them over. And this can be applied to all areas of your life. Conversations can be truly inspiring if we open up and show true interest in the people we are talking to.

The following are sixteen questions that are guaranteed to make for more interesting conversations in your day-to-day life. They will take most people by surprise and will generate their interest. See if you can challenge yourself to remember just one of these questions. Then, start experimenting with your conversational opportunities in life:

1. If happiness were the national currency, what kind of work would make you rich?
2. If the average human life span was forty years, how would you live your life differently?
3. If you could offer a newborn baby only one piece of advice, what would it be?
4. What is the one thing you'd most like to change about the world?
5. What is one thing you have not done that you really want to do? And what's holding you back?
6. Would you break the law to save a loved one?
7. Have you ever seen insanity where you later saw creativity?
8. What's something you do differently than most people?
9. Do you push the elevator button more than once? Do you really believe it makes the elevator faster?
10. What are you most grateful for?
11. What is your greatest fear?
12. Have you ever been with someone, said nothing, and walked away feeling like you just had the best conversation ever?

13. If you just won a million dollars, would you quit your job? Why don't you quit already if you would quit if you had a million dollars?

14. Would you be willing to reduce your life expectancy by ten years to become extremely attractive or famous?

15. What is the difference between being alive and truly living?

16. What would you do differently if you knew nobody would judge you?

Reflection

I grew up playing basketball. I was one of the top players in San Diego my senior year in high school. I was considered the most valuable player of one of the top leagues in Southern California, and thought I would go on to play college basketball. I played my whole life and worked as hard as I could. I was given numerous opportunities to play basketball in college. But when I decided to go, I realized that playing wasn't fulfilling me anymore. It didn't feel like it was what I was supposed to do. Every single day felt like drudgery. Although I believe that at times we have to do things we don't want to do (like sometimes I don't like sitting down and writing), it was different with basketball because it always felt like drudgery. It didn't start out like that, but as it got more serious, and turned into work in order for me to stay in school, I lost my passion for it. I started to find interest in other things, such as traveling, and ultimately I decided to quit school and basketball to travel.

I went in a completely different direction. I started backpacking around the world, I grew my hair out long, and I quit going to the gym every day. Well, in reality, I quit going to the gym altogether.

If someone were to look at me now, they may assume that I am the anti-jock. I have really long hair, I'm kind of skinny, and I write books. I also do yoga and enjoy meditating.

But, in reality, sports have made me who I am today. It took me a while to realize this. It actually happened recently when I was having a phone call with my agent, Bill Gladstone. He asked about the influence that sports had on my life, and it was a question that no one had ever asked me before. People ask me often if I still play basketball, but they never ask me what I had learned from playing. His question was so profound that it caused me to reflect in a way that I hadn't before. At the end of my time playing basketball competitively, I had lost all interest and was so unhappy that I had blocked the entire experience out. I hadn't really thought about why I felt the way I did or why I loved basketball in the first place.

I was never the best athlete. In basketball, there were always people who were more physically gifted than I was, who jumped higher than I did, and who were stronger than I was. But I was almost always team captain and one of the best players on the court. It wasn't because of my physical abilities—it was because I always dove for the loose ball. Even if there was no chance of getting it, I still dove for it. I was also a shooter and I was one of the top three-point shooters in San Diego. I made it where I was because of my work ethic.

I think I learned this work ethic from my father. I remember that while in middle school and high school I would wake up at two or three in the morning to go to the restroom and I would look out my window, and would notice that my dad's office light was still on. He had been working through the night. A lot of his business was done overseas, and so at night here was when a lot of his clients were awake in other parts of the world. He did computer work in America during the day, and at night he worked with people in other countries. And despite how hard he worked, he still taught me how to play sports, and was able to be there for me as a father figure.

I never really noticed it at the time, but now when I think about it I realize that I never had to worry about having a roof over my head or food to eat because my dad worked really hard. So when I decided to write a book, with no credentials and a very limited number of people who believed in me, I thought about my dad. I figured that if I never give up, and work as hard as I possibly can, like my dad, I will be a successful author and live my dream. But this will only happen if I work as hard as I possibly can—which at times may mean sleepless nights, and extreme imbalance.

When thinking about how I will be able to make my dreams a reality, I also need to remember everything I learned from sports. One of the most important things I learned was how to set routines. When I walked to the free-throw line and shot a three-pointer, I shot the same way every time. My knees, elbows, and feet were positioned in the same way, and my hand followed through the same way every time. I also held the ball in the same spot, with my fingertips, every shot.

I can apply similar habits to writing. Diving for every loose ball proved that as a basketball player I played as hard as I could every day. I was someone the team could count on. Now I am learning to channel that follow-through energy in a different way. Instead of being the guy who dives for all the loose balls, I'm the guy who gets to where he needs to be on time to any event (even if I am tired). Also, when my favorite publishing company rejected me, I could have quit. But because of the way I am, I realized that if I quit I wouldn't have been able to live my dream. Writing and speaking is my dream, and playing sports gave me a level of tenacity that has allowed me to get the most out of myself on the court, in writing, and in life.

I'm very thankful for having played sports and I am glad my agent asked me this question so that I could realize how much they taught me. There are many experiences in our lives that we do not look back at to reflect on. We learn things in life that help us stay positive, that help us understand and observe other people, and that help shape who we become—and often we don't realize why we are the way we are. We forget that much of the way we look at the world has been learned. Even when we are tired of doing something or experiencing something we must take time to reflect and be grateful for what we have learned from doing it. Most of the time, we learn from the things we have done and they have helped shape us into stronger human beings. The more you reflect upon what you have learned from the experiences in your life—be they boring, ecstatic, happy, sad, or terrifying—the more you will grow and evolve.

Money

> Making money isn't hard in itself . . . what's hard is to earn it doing something worth devoting one's life to.
>
> —Carlos Ruiz Zafón, Spanish novelist

Everything is energy, including money. It's what you do with energy that makes it positive or negative, as it has no inherent polarity. People often say, "Look how much stress and tension money causes, it affects our daily lives negatively. It's evil." People are quick to label money as evil, but they often forget that it's not the energy that is evil, it's your relationship with it. Even poor relationships with food can make some people so overweight that they die from eating it. But food isn't evil.

The truth is anything, including money, food, and medicine, can be used in an irresponsible way. People can be greedy and act violently for all types of things including money, sex, power, television, shopping, food, jobs, and more. And often having money can cause just as much stress as not having it does. But this doesn't have to be the case.

Money is a medium to measure value and you need to try to have a positive relationship with money to use its advantages. It can help you get higher-quality food, water, shelter, and clothes; it can give you the ability to travel, help others, invest in projects, and reach new goals. Having money minimizes stress. Money can help make you more of what you are—generous or selfish.

People often have a misconception that rich people are greedy and bad. But this isn't always the case. I have met mega-millionaires who were some of the most generous people I've ever met. I've met people who have more money than they can ever spend and they were extremely nice and happy people. And, on the other hand, I have met people who had more than enough money and were not very generous or kind at all.

Money simply makes people more of who they are. If someone is scared all the time, and they get a bunch of money, it's not going to take away their fear. In fact, they will probably use their money to perpetuate their fears and it will show in very obvious ways (hoarding it, unnecessary alarm systems, lots of spending on safety devices, and valuing experiences simply by how much they cost). If someone is greedy, they will continue to hoard, and money will not make them feel less greedy. Money gives us the opportunity to be more of who we are because it gives us more energy. And it is your intention for its use that makes money a negative or positive medium in your life.

Money can give us the freedom to focus on what we love to do. It takes away the fear that stops many of us when we feel that we don't have the resources we need. It can help you get what you need to build your dreams, in terms of resources. People block themselves from receiving money because they say that it's evil, but then they stress about not having it and not having the right resources. Instead of wasting time worrying about whether or not money is evil, why not use our time to live our passion and see what happens if we make money doing it? Having money can help us influence the world in a much more positive way than complaining about those who have it.

Just because someone trips over their shoelaces and breaks their arm doesn't mean that shoelaces are bad and that we should never wear them again. Also, just because some people have crashed cars or other people steal cars doesn't mean that cars are evil. It's not the money that is the problem—it's how you use it or what you think you need to do to get it that is the problem.

Believing that you can't make enough money doing what you love is also a huge mistake. There are plenty of people who make a lot of money doing just what they love. In fact, many of the people who I have mentioned throughout this book make more than they need doing exactly what they love. Money will come if you follow your heart.

Money should be a means to an end, not the end. If you become addicted to simply making more money, then you will lose your center and you will probably not use money in a healthy way. Think of money as a tool that helps you have more freedom and interesting experiences, and helps you build your dreams.

Think about your relationship with money and why you want it. Examining your intentions will help you determine if you need to make any adjustments to how you relate to it. Being honest with yourself about your relationship with money can help you craft a healthier life and is an exercise that can be applied to all relationships in your life. Allow your relationship with money to improve your life (along with your relationships with all people, places, and things). See it as a blessing to earn it doing what you love. The more you make, the more you can give.

Chapter 15

Ask for What You Want

Ask for what you want and be prepared to get it!

—MAYA ANGELOU

Many times when we ask for what we want subconsciously, we ask in a negative way. This matters because everything we say transmits an image to the person we say it to. For example, if we ask for what we want by saying, "If it wouldn't trouble you *too* much, maybe, *please*, will you be able to help me? *Please*. I really need your help." While asking that way might get us what we want, it sends a negative message to our subconscious and hinders our ability to receive it more than it helps us.

When our minds receive a question, they instantly start to analyze the question. Then, about half a second later, our minds produce images related to the question. Since our minds work in this way, the language that we use to ask for things is really important. You need to program your subconscious mind in a more expansive way when asking questions—don't sound desperate or as though you are begging for something to happen.

Jack Canfield gives great explanations about how to ask for what you want. He explains that if you ask the question: *How can I have this? How can I do this?* Then the person you are asking will start questioning, too. They will think: *Well, how can I help make this a reality for this person?*

When I heard Jack explain this concept I thought that it was very interesting. I vowed to myself that when the opportunity presented itself, I would test his theory out. Then, the opportunity came. I heard about a big speaking expo and I wanted to speak at it. However, I found out about it only one month before the event. The event programming was completely finished, they had all their speakers lined up, and everything was ready to go. Then, a good friend of mine was able to set up a phone call for me with one of the event planners of the expo. When we got on the phone, the man received me with a lot of excitement. He was thrilled with the work I was doing, and he really loved my message. He had checked out my book and my website, and was so excited. However, there was still one big problem—they had already set up the event nine months in advance, none of the speakers had dropped out, and they had no more budget to bring someone else on. "Well, you know, Jake, we would love to have you the following year. And maybe we can work out ways where we can partner up in the near future. What you're doing is so great, and we are so excited about it! Seriously. Do you have any questions? Comments?" he said to me. "Well," I replied, "I do have a question. How would it be possible for me to speak at *this* event? I really believe I can speak at this event. How can I *please* speak at it?"

He was silent for a moment. "Well, I may have an idea. Let me give you a call in a little bit." Then I told him about other people that worked to assist me, such as my booking manager, and gave him his contact information. I got a text message from him later, saying that the head event coordinator wanted to have a phone call with my manager. I left for the weekend, and when I returned on Monday morning, my manager called, "Guess what? You are not going to believe this, but you got the spot for this speech, *and* you are going to be giving the keynote speech, too!"

All I could do was smile and laugh. It was the first time I had ever tried to ask for something respectfully, but in a totally positive manner. *How can I speak at this event? How can I?* When the mind asks that question to someone else, it in turn asks the question back to itself. How can I? So when I asked this person, he thought immediately in his head, *How can I help Jake speak at this event?* And his mind immediately figured out the answer unconsciously. Remember that, consciously, he had told me that I wasn't able to speak at the event.

When you ask questions, you trigger people's unconscious mind. Because I had stated my question in a double positive, the result was positive. Try it out for yourself! How can I *please* have this now? *How* would it please be possible for this to happen? Test it out, and see how it goes for you, and from now on be aware of the ways in which you ask questions.

SWSWSWSW

> Some people fold after making one timid request. They quit too soon. Keep asking until you find the answers. There are usually four or five "no"s before you get a "yes."
>
> —Jack Canfield

If you believe in what you want, you have to ask for what you want. If you believe in something, you have to stand for it or else you can never stand in freedom. If you want something, and you believe in it, you have to go out and get it.

It's important to remember something that Jack Canfield teaches, which he calls SWSWSWSW. It stands for *Some Will Some Won't So What Someone's Waiting*. Some will say yes when you ask for what you want, someone will want to help you, someone will want to buy your product, someone will want to help your cause, some will say yes, and some will say no. Some will be nice about it and some will be mean and disrespectful. Some will and some won't. Some will say yes and some will say no. And so what? Keep asking.

Jack really empowered me when I was working on my first book because a lot of agents and publishers told me "No." Jack says that whenever someone says "No" you say *next*. (And no, it doesn't have to be out loud; you can say it to yourself.) If you want something, and you ask, and someone says "No"—then so what? Go to the next person, because someone else is waiting. Yes, that's right, someone is *waiting* to help you. Someone *wants* to help someone like you, so just ask if they can help you. Don't be too scared about what happens. If you really want something, you should never stop asking for it. The difference between someone who lives a mediocre life and someone who lives an extraordinary life is that the people who live extraordinarily never stop asking for what they want. But this doesn't change the fact that sometimes life has a plan of its own. We may not get exactly what we want, but sometimes that can be a great strike of luck. Remember, ask for *this or something better*. As long as you keep moving forward with positive persistence, the right thing will happen for you.

I will remind you again that I had always wanted my first book, *Into the Wind*, to be published by a certain company. All my favorite authors got their books published by them, so my only focus was that *they* would publish my book. I wrote it all over my journal, and I told myself that it would happen all the time. (And I literally mean *all* the time.) I even taped a poster of getting my book published with them on my wall.

Then, when I finished my book, I really thought that they would take it because I had met some people in the company. However, when I sent in my proposal, they said "No," they told me to self-publish it with their self-publishing division instead, which I immediately took great offense to. But it all turned out okay. I am young and very passionate—I sold my first book on my own, went on tour, and inspired lots of people. And ultimately, we found a publisher and it turned out better than I could have imagined. The book you are reading has been published by Penguin Random House, the largest publisher in the world, which I never would have imagined being possible.

This story is a perfect example of why it's important to remember that when we get faced with a "No," it's often because something else bigger and better is opening up for us. I'm happier than I ever could have imagined. Everything works out in the end. So ask for what you want, be persistent, and stay positive. In the end you will receive what you deserve.

Persistence

You create your opportunities by asking for them.

—Patty Hansen

Taylor Swift, a young country singer who has won just about every award imaginable and who has touched the lives of hundreds of millions of people throughout the world, would never have gotten on our radar if she hadn't asked for what she wanted. When she was sixteen, she had a mixtape and she wanted to be the opening act for singer Tim McGraw. She contacted him and he said, "I don't even use an opening act." But she kept calling him every day for two weeks, and he ended up telling her to stop annoying him. Then, one day, he finally went ahead and listened to her mixtape. He called a few weeks later, and just like that, her career was launched. She was on tour with Tim McGraw.

We see Swift singing onstage, breaking records with her songs, touching lives, and living a life of success. She is a great example for us all, but we forget to look at her path and see how she got there. Her path to living her dream started the same way that anyone else's starts. In fact, it started the same way that yours must start—by asking for what you want.

How to Live Your Dreams

You can't ask for what you want unless you know what it is. A lot of people don't know what they want or they want much less than they deserve. First, you have to figure out what you want. Second, you have to decide that you deserve it. Third, you have to believe you can get it. And fourth, you have to have the guts to ask for it.

—Barbara De Angelis

Ask the universe for what you want and be clear about it. If you have something you can share with the world, or if you just want something in your day-to-day life, like better communication skills, better relationships, or whatever it may be, just *ask*. So often we get scared to ask for what we want. *Well, I don't want to be pushy with that person. You know, I just don't know if I really even want it that bad, you know, it doesn't matter that much anyways. They might be busy and I just don't want to ask them because they might say no. What if it makes them mad? Yeah, I don't know. It's not that big of a deal. It doesn't matter that much. . . .*

Does any of that sound familiar? That's how I always used to talk to myself. Until one day, when I realized that literally the worst thing that could happen is ending up exactly where I was before I asked. You will not go backward if someone says no when you need to ask for what you want. If worse comes to worst, you will simply end up right where you already were—so why not ask? No matter what it is, no matter what you want to do, you are going to have to *ask* for it. And you are going to have to ask for other things to help you achieve what it is you are asking for. If you have a dream about doing something, but don't ask for it because you have over-rationalized it, or have come up with some sort of excuse about why you can't ask, you are only harming yourself.

As human beings, it is natural for us to feel a desire and act upon it. But to act upon and realize a desire, or to live the way we want, we need to be courageous and ask for things. So, if you've been waiting to ask someone to partner up with you in business, for a loan, for help; to go up to that person you find attractive; or to ask someone to go on a run with you, *stop* waiting. Whether it is something related to work, relationships, health, friendship, or basic human needs, just ask!

The more you can make it a habit to ask for what you want, the more the sunrise of your confidence begins to shine—and the constant heaviness in your body and mind from consistently neglecting to ask fades away. It's not rude to ask for what you want. If you want something, ask somebody. Ask them in a respectful way, and be mindful about who they are, what they have, and where they are coming from. And just because they are coming from a different place from you, or you think they might be, that isn't a reason *not* to ask. All roads eventually intersect at some point.

If you have been kicking yourself because you constantly see individuals that you find attractive, yet you don't walk over to talk to them and ask for their number, or at least for their name, stop selling yourself short. If you need an investment to start your dream and have been scared to ask, *ask!* You literally have no reason not to. I think most of the regrets in our life come not from being rejected, but from rejecting ourselves and never asking for what we want.

Ask for what you want. Ask how to get where you want to be. Live your dreams. (You won't be sorry.)

ACKNOWLEDGMENTS

This book wouldn't have been possible without the love and support of Jack and Inga Canfield. I appreciate all that you have done for me. Thank you for being a part of my life.

When I received the contract for this book from Penguin, I called my literary agent, Bill Gladstone, and started crying. I couldn't really talk because I was crying too hard. I owe a lot to him and I would like to acknowledge him for everything he's done for me (which includes too many things to list).

A special thank-you goes out to one of my editors, Tara Gladstone. She took the first crack at my rough manuscript and has made it into something beautiful. Thank you.

I would also like to heartily acknowledge Jeremy Tarcher; my publisher, Joel Fotinos; and the rest of the Penguin Random House team. Thank you for believing in me at such a young age. You've made one of my dreams come true. I'd also like to add a special word of appreciation for Andrew Yackira, my editor at Penguin, for his excitement in the project as well.

Additionally, I want to thank Amish Shah for believing in me, and for helping take my message and vision to the next level. I can't wait for what the future holds. . . . And thank you to Jason Moffat for introducing Amish and me.

All my respect also goes to Jennifer Lasek and Brian Gadinsky—I love the two of you!

Last, but not least, I'd like to praise everyone who is mentioned in this book. Your stories have inspired me, and that is why I have shared them with the world. If I haven't met you in person, I hope to be graced with the opportunity one day. You've changed my life.